Holding faith

Holding faith

creating peace in a violent world

David Gee

QUAKERbooks

Published in July 2011 by Quaker Books
Friends House, Euston Road, London NW1 2BJ
publications@quaker.org.uk

ISBN: 978 1 907123 19 1
Design & typesetting by Gabrielle Scott
Cover design by Quaker Communications
Cover image: 'Pale Blue Window' by Sarah Gittins
Text typeface: Minion Pro 11/14
Printed by Ashford colour press
Registered charity number 1127633
www.quaker.org.uk

Epigraph by Ben Okri from *A way of being free*. London: Phoenix, 1997.

'...their choice is dictated by the quality of their love...'

Ben Okri

For my parents, Margaret and Sam, who loved enough

Contents

1

Choosing peace

Fifteen years ago I was one of five thousand people taking part in a demonstration against the new M77 motorway, whose route was cutting through ancient woodland near Glasgow. The march led from the humdrum bustle of the city centre, out into the countryside to the threshold between the half-built motorway's path and the forest.

It was dusk by the time we arrived. The place was on a hill and there were views of miles around. From the far horizon the motorway snaked towards us, a familiar alien ripping through the land. There was such power there. On the other side the protesters, who had been living in the forest for months, were clambering over the limbs of the trees. There was power here, too; a kind of passion for life. They get called 'protesters' – people with a complaint to make – but first of all they are believers.

I felt caught between these two realities; one of that creative passion that flows from life and dignifies us, and the other a kind of sprawling presumption of entitlement to the world. In that moment I felt pressed to choose between them. I had either to stand with life and the living world or dumbly acquiesce to the road's brash violation of it.

This dualistic and emotionally charged response to the road and the forest seems romantically simplistic now. Nonetheless, its essential truth still resonates: that a tension between the free abundance and integrity of life on the one hand and a hollow thoughtlessness that violates life on the other, runs right through the drama of the world and everyone in it.

Peace as the dignity of being

We owe the word 'peace' to the Latin *pax*, meaning agreement (cf. 'pact') and derived from the Indo-European root *pag*, meaning 'fetter': something held down or back. From this comes the everyday sense of peace, defined in the negative as a state or place clear of disturbance or volatility. But the biblical Hebrew word *shalom* (Arabic *salaam*), meaning something like 'wholeness', is also rendered in English as 'peace'. Unlike the 'peace' of *pax*, *shalom* is associated with wholeness, abundance, health, well-being – the integrity of our common aliveness. Biblical uses of *shalom* imply a sense of the dignity and vibrancy of our being flourishing *as it should*, which demands not to be violated.

The peace of *shalom* abounds almost anywhere we choose to look. It is there in the procession of seasons, the intricacies of ecosystems and the precise migrations of birds. It is even there in the laws of physics, simple, fecund and mysterious as they are. The love between parents and children, between friends and for welcoming strangers, and in kids who can turn any spare nook or cranny into a place to play, all testify to the ubiquity of peace as *shalom*. In these things the dignity of our being affirms itself.

Yet around our aliveness, not as part of it, we persistently violate one another, our ecological neighbourhood and ourselves. A concern for the dignity of one another's being is plainly not always leading our choices, nor is it axiomatic in the economic, political, cultural systems we participate in. The global capitalist consensus that powerfully shapes our societies allows the richest 80 people in the world to hold the same collective wealth as the poorest third of the population earns in a year.[1] Here again are two worlds in one: life's integrity and abundance on one hand and on the other its persistent violation. Whether or not we realise it, we create these two worlds in the choices we make every day and also in how societies are organised.

Peace as truthfulness

The authenticity of our humanity is at stake in the choices we make as individuals, communities and societies. From a peace-making point of view, how truthful we are being to ourselves is reflected in how well, with good faith, we create peace and stand against violence. To choose peace, then, is to bend towards a relationship with the world that allows fundamental needs to be met in life-giving rather than life-destroying ways, and to work for a society in which that choice becomes more possible to make. In this light, a commitment to peace is not so much an add-on for a good life, nor an ideological view about the moral failure of violence, but a practical expression of a feeling for what life and society are really about.

Met with violence, our authenticity is tested: will we stand with life in the face of its violation? For every 'for' there is an 'against'. The M77 protesters are doing more than protecting the forest and what it means for them; they are also opposing the life-destroying forces and norms that the motorway represents. Yet the choice between peace and violence, life and death, is not always an obvious one. If the motorway is symptomatic of our collective spiritual and ecological myopia it is still someone's creative project: it generates work; there is an honest feeling of accomplishment when the job is complete; and now most of us use it as if it had always been there.

So in committing to peace there is an authentically necessary confrontation, but it is not between the 'good guys' and the 'bad guys', which is a convenient conceit, but between life and the violation of life – between peace and violence. The motorway may not be part of the peace but its engineer is. In standing for peace and against violence, we might stand against what the engineer is doing and not against him as a person. Nonetheless, we are still taking sides.

As the dignity of our being, peace is both received – it is in the fabric of the universe – and created in the choices we make. Peace-making depends on the authenticity of the relationship we as individuals and societies choose to have with the world: how it dignifies our common being or violates it. Consider this statement by the Quaker John Lynes:

> What shook me was a map of the world. In black were the principal arms-exporting nations – in red were the areas where major wars had been fought since 1945. The black and the red areas did not overlap. This was my road to Damascus. Then and there I saw where my choice lay; with the Crucified or with the crucifiers.[2]

When most of us see such a map we might spend a moment to lament a violent world and pop a few coins in a pot marked 'Donations'. John, in contrast, is left viscerally shaken as if he has seen the world for the first time. Through his experience of the map the violence of the arms trade is communicated with unusual power. This has taken him to a turning point, at which a choice is demanded of him about nothing less than how he will live.

By using the symbols of a faith story, John invites us to imagine our way into the meaning of his experience. In likening the modern trade in arms to the Crucifixion, he identifies the human devastation of a business that thrives on war with the violation of a guiltless man nearly 2,000 years ago. His words challenge their reader to further connect the two phenomena as violations of a kind that are pre-meditated, indulgent, legally sanctioned and socially convenient. Like the people who came to watch the crucifixion of Jesus, the arms trade has its casual onlookers – people who stop for a while to gaze at the map and then walk on. But John is held. Were he to walk on from the map, he would be complicit with the crucifiers. Instead, he is pressed to stand with the crucified: with Jesus the peace-maker and with all those affected by war. His authenticity is being tested and he cannot ignore, dodge or forget the choice that faces him without radically diminishing who he is as a human being. His commitment to living truthfully has become inseparable from a commitment to peace-making.

John's language of story and symbol belongs to what Walter Brueggemann calls the 'prophetic imagination'.[3] It is a way of seeing (and being in) the world that reaches beyond the bare facts to apprehend something of their meaning as a whole. Those who believe Jesus was the one son of a creator God will interpret John's statement in light of that belief. Those who do not can nonetheless get a sense of its meaning. Whatever our beliefs may be, unless we as readers push the question away entirely we cannot help but ask where we stand: with the crucifying structures of the arms trade or the peace-making crucified and all those who suffer in war. Whatever the Christian story means to us, and however much or little we might feel involved in it, John's statement puts us all on the hook.

'Shaken'

John wrote, "What shook me…" and then, "…I saw where my choice lay…". The theologian Andrew Shanks speculates that such "shakenness" generates the conditions of greater authenticity, by which new, life-affirming social movements may occur. He explains that the philosopher Jan Patočka first used the term to describe Charter 77, the underground movement that seeded popular resistance to the Soviet domination of Czechoslovakia. The movement's founding declaration, which Patočka signed, describes it as "a free, informal and open association of people of different convictions, different faiths and different professions".[4] It appealed not to people's existing religious or political views but to something more elemental: their common situation as human beings whose freedom had been stolen. By the risky method of *samizdat*, by which activists clandestinely copied and passed on the outlawed declaration, the movement grew. Over two decades later it culminated in the almost entirely non-violent Velvet Revolution of 1989 when another founding figure of Charter 77, the writer Václav Havel, was inaugurated as the first President of the Czech Republic.

Andrew Shanks explains that in describing the Charter 77 signatories as "shaken", Jan Patočka referred to their common experience of being jolted into an authentic, passionate response to the violence of their situation.[5] Their shakenness began to move them away from living "within a lie" – their complicity with the regime – and towards living "within the truth", which is to say a more honest way of being.[6] Just as importantly, they drew together into what Patočka called the "solidarity of the shaken".[7] In this, Shanks argues, lies the critical importance of shakenness for the birth and growth of new social movements, as "the shaken" seek one another out as allies and friends. In the case of movements like Charter 77, and perhaps also the Quaker movement, people are being drawn together in their common shakenness, committed to living more authentically and being more deeply engaged in the world. For these, such commitment is a life choice rather than a lifestyle choice.

The shaken might well belong to a religious denomination, organisation or political party. Their first loyalty, however, is to being a *movement* of common solidarity in a shared feeling for what is authentic and powerful enough to move society away from a lie towards truth. And the shaken, in being passionate, are radicalised; they are people of the *radix*, or root, of life. A measure of our organisations, including Quaker ones, is how well they serve this loose movement of gathered and gathering people working to turn themselves and the world around.

Turning around

The turn towards peace, initiated by the shakenness that John Lynes and Andrew Shanks describe, is a small revolution from which grows larger, slower evolutionary change. The biblical Greek term for this kind of revolution-evolution is *metanoia*. Although normally translated into English as 'repentance', as in remorse for sin, *metanoia* means something like the 'turning-around' of life and the world. Quakers call this experience 'convincement', based on the early Quaker term 'convicted', meaning found guilty of one's sin and turned around towards a new kind of life. For Quakers, like many other religious communities, faith concerns this turning away from life within a lie towards a newly felt authenticity. It is made real (or not) by how we act in the world.

Metanoia has a private, spiritual dimension but its purpose is practical and emancipatory. I saw it in a harassed single mum at a parenting group who started to kneel down when talking to her toddler, trying to enter his world for a few minutes each day. It was there, too, when a soldier friend decided the war in Iraq was wrong, left the army and started to wake the rest of us up to the reality of war. And when a woman who fell into a rage and beat someone up, her *metanoia* was to find help; she pinned a diagram of nonviolence principles on her fridge door as a daily reminder. These were not isolated changes but signs of lives turning around as each person moved into what they described in their own words as more authentic and life-giving ways of being in the world. Such mini-revolutions are how the world begins to change.

If our own *metanoia* is inevitably inconsistent – because we are lax and this sort of change does not proceed in a rationally ordered way – then it is not surprising that our social, collective *metanoia* from violence to peace is so slow and uncertain, if indeed it is happening at all. However, it is well within our power to be an influence by participating in the processes of change and sometimes giving the social tree a shake. And this works. In the eighteenth century, the American John Woolman travelled among his own slave-owning Quaker community and challenged them gently but persistently on the inconsistency between what they were professing and what they were doing. He endured repeated "yes, but…" responses until eventually the penny dropped and Quakers began releasing their slaves and campaigning together for abolition. One *metanoia* leads to another.

Peace as commitment

A commitment to peace in the sense described here concerns a determination to respect the dignity of one another's being in the way we live, commune and organise our societies. More than a critique of violence, then, a peace commitment is first a passion for the promise of life. It means searching for an authentic relationship with others, working to re-create the world as fit for flourishing relationships, and resolving to resist and refuse the multiple violations of violence. In other words, it is a way of holding faith with life and making this count in a pervasively violent world.

The word 'commitment' originally meant 'bringing together', and in this sense a commitment to peace focuses the will, marshals our resources and brings us together in the same passion for the dignity and vibrancy of being alive. These choices have a profoundly ethical dimension in that they have consequences in the world also. Yet they are more than this, for they lead to larger and deeper freedom of being. The M77 activists drew together in hope of not only a more ethical society but one that is more alive; I see them not so much as the righteous but as the alive. So peace is a matter of both the ethical integrity of our choices and of the passion, freedom and communion in which they are made. In this way, a commitment to peace leads into what the Quaker Adrian Rose calls a "greater embrace"[8] of our riven, beautiful world: to be a little more unsettled, engaged and alive.

2

Having faith

Re-imagining faith

As the first chapter suggested, a commitment to peace is a humane passion played out in the world. At the same time, what Ben Okri has said of the poet might also be true of the peace-maker:

> [They] must draw to themselves heaven's aid, for their calling is absorbing and demanding, rigorous as conscience and elusive as freedom.[9]

Here is an intimation that we will struggle unless we realise that the power that makes peace comes not only from within us but from around us as well. Whether literally or metaphorically the gods stand ready to participate with us in the peace-making journey. To this end, this chapter suggests that a humane, critically aware faith can help to hold and deepen a commitment to the dignity of our common being.

Faith is what you trust in

Although the word 'faith' is often associated with holding a specific belief, it comes from the Latin word *fidere*, meaning 'to trust'. The trust involved in Quaker worship and work is not in having the right belief about 'God' but in desiring and waiting for heaven's aid to work through hearts and minds so that all our humanity is deepened. The preoccupations of this kind of faith are therefore mainly existential – questions of how we live – rather than ontological – questions of what exists.

Many people who do not identify with a religious tradition seem wary even of others' faith. When friends and acquaintances have asked me about Quakers and I have explained the Christian roots of the movement, they have often asked, "Ah, so do you believe in God?" They mean, do I believe that a Judaeo-Christian God exists and – did they flinch? – the question behind the question is typically, "Bit of a weirdo, are you?" Yet a simple yes/no answer would tacitly accept the assumptions in the question: that faith is all about believing that God exists, that faith is based on having a correct belief about God, and that faith is just a bit bonkers. The dominant public debate on religion inadvertently reinforces those assumptions. In 2009, an atheist group commissioned an advertisement on the side of a bus:

> There's probably no God. Now stop worrying and enjoy your life.

A Christian group quickly retaliated:

> There definitely is a God. So join the Christian Party and enjoy your life.

How did these groups become so sure about the gods? It confuses belief with knowledge to claim beyond doubt that there definitely is a God; and despite the "clear thinking oasis" that Richard Dawkins' website claims to be, no science can drum up odds for God's non-existence.[10] Our "moonlit and dream-visited planet", as William James described it, is too fuzzy for probable or definite claims about the gods.[11] Faith as trust, by contrast, is the profoundly human concern of what we do when we *don't* know.

Before it is anything else, faith is first a search for a meaningful response to our situation in the world, and for this we need more than rational intellect alone, just as we would not rely on scientific method to appreciate a poem. We understand and respond using our whole being: by reason, certainly, but also by our creative imagination and what Iain Crichton Smith called "the feeling intelligence"[12] Without imagination and feeling there would be no faith – and the sceptic would be happy with that. But there would also be none of the arts, nor love, and we would also not know how to laugh, all of which are meaningful forms of understanding and response to the world. In terms of the wonderings of faith, explanation-loving reason might ponder whether 'God' exists, while symbol-loving imagination ponders what 'God' might mean. If we think we have to settle the first question before exploring the second, we are bound to get stuck there as the bus ads have.

The association of the word 'true' with 'factually correct' did not exist, as far as we know, before the mid-sixteenth century, and it only became the term's dominant sense during the Enlightenment. This is recent history for most religious traditions. Earlier, the Old English *triewe* meant trustworthy, as in something or someone we could have faith in. Our starting point does not have to be knowing just what's what about the gods; it can be acceptance that we are all at sea and need to discover what is worth trusting in and acting upon. This kind of faith is less like following a perfect map of the world, more like beseeching the stars' help through the night and knowing that we need their heavenly aid.

Trust is a matter of degree; it is possible to trust too much or too little. Some Judaeo-Christian teaching instructs us to do whatever God commands, for we should trust divine wisdom even if we do not fully understand it. This view follows the story of Abraham, whose faith was so resolute that he was prepared to sacrifice Isaac, his only son, when God demanded it. At its worst, however, such obedience reduces faith to a game of *Simon Says*. In this case, the relationship with God has no mutuality – no push-and-pull, resist-and-relent tussle that testifies to a relationship in which we are genuinely ready to be disturbed and changed. At the other end of this spectrum is a sort of fair-weather faith of cherry-picking whichever bits of a religious tradition seem to be "underlining in red whatever you happen to be feeling", as Rowan Williams has put it.[13] In this, too, there is no mutuality, only a loveless marriage of convenience between ourselves and the Godself.

Somewhere between these extremes is an approach to faith that starts with listening for a felt sense of 'God'. Meanings of 'God' are then discovered as part of a journey, rather than something we know before we set off. The first of the *Advices and queries* used by British Quakers reads: "Take heed, dear Friends, to the promptings of Love and Truth in your hearts. Trust them as the leadings of God whose Light shows us our darkness and brings us to new life." Quakers believe that we encounter a relationship with God in everyday life by trusting the impulse to be truthful and to love, and so the meaning of 'God' is found first in the listening hearts and minds of a faith community. The relationship to 'God' is of neither blind obedience nor self-centred expediency. Rather, the journey is of honest wondering, being disturbed and changed but never taken away from our own humanity. This kind of passionate, exploratory faith can bring us more deeply into life, as long as we don't wriggle off the hook it puts us on.

The Quaker founder George Fox said that what he knew, he knew 'experimentally', meaning that he found his truth by experience rather than by reading it in a holy book or by hearing it from a priest. It is perhaps characteristic of Quakers both to believe that experience is the prime arbiter of truth and, at the same time, that we do not know what we do not know. Yet for early Quakers and many other people of faith, both then and since, to know experimentally also meant to have the conviction of a strong, critically aware feeling for what is true.

Faith is a revolution

It is risky to talk about faith traditions en masse but, tentatively speaking, religions are typically concerned with what makes our relationship with the world and its gods 'right'. When a Muslim prays five times a day, a right relationship with the world and with Allah is being made; indeed, the rightness of the relationship depends on whether and how the prayers are offered.

Fundamental to the rightness of relationship, so faith traditions typically insist, is that something other than our egos comes before us in the universal pecking order. As Karen Armstrong puts it, faith "de-thrones" us from the centre of our own lives for the sake of whatever we have chosen to trust in.[14] For Abrahamic religions this is God; for some pagans it is the living Earth; for some Hindus, Brahman, Shiva or Vishnu; for some Buddhists it is not a god or a principle but the no-thing of *sunyata*. By challenging us to step down voluntarily from the centre of our universe, a faith discipline seeks to turn our lives the right way up and then supports us to live in that inverted state. In so doing, faith aims for a revolution first in our hearts and then, from there, in the world.

By this faith-led inversion of the universe, the personal becomes political. In India, for example, Gandhian activists are campaigning to stop the state parcelling up land to sell to multinational corporations. People whose families have worked the fields for generations are being summarily evicted for want of a piece of paper proving prior ownership.

The activists see what the corporations do not. Our lives come from the land and depend on it; it gives us not only what we need to live, but the very possibility of living. We belong to the land, not the other way around, and so it is not for us to use up and dispose of as we like. They see that if we treat the Earth only as a commodity – that is, as a possession that we are entitled to trade – then we see it as less than it really is, which cannot but compromise it as a source of life. The error in commodifying the land is therefore not just in failing to give it due care, it is also in forgetting that it comes before us.

According to P. V. Rajagopal, the activists have a chant about the land, beginning: "It is not mine, it is not yours…"[15] In these few words the activists declare that the land, while there for us to use is not for us to possess. The chant continues: "…it is God's." By this, they declare that the land is sacred, meaning that it comes before us in the universe. If you put yourself before the land, the activists imply, then you violate the Earth and God. Often, 'sacred' implies taboo: something we must not touch or somewhere we should not tread, such as an area of a religious building reserved for a priestly class. The land, in contrast, is for all life to participate in, yet as a sacred thing it is still off limits in that it has no price and cannot be possessed as a commodity or measured like one. It is an end in itself.

For now it does not matter whether the activists are thinking of God as Vishnu, Shiva, Krishna or Ganesh, nor does it matter what we understand by God when we hear the chant. We do not have to believe (although we might) that a particular deity exists, with a specific name and nature. For now, 'God' is a word that enables the activists to talk about the land as sacred, declaring that it is beyond any human claim to ownership.

In the few words of their chant the activists demonstrate the political power of a passion held in faith. India's now dominant political model, based like our own on perpetual economic growth, presumes an entitlement to commodify the land. The activists' chant, made possible by a feeling for what is sacred, succinctly exposes this system as a violation of humanity, the Earth and God. The immediate problems they face with the state and the corporations are seen to have a deep structure which reflects the relationship that human beings are making with the world.

Like John Lynes, the Indian land activists are concerned with searching for, and holding with, a right relationship with the world and with their God. The dignity of humanity and the Earth is merged inseparably with that of their God. One way of understanding this is that 'God', as a term of faith, becomes real by what we do in love of humanity and the Earth. Carter Heyward writes:

> From an experiential standpoint – that is, from within the experience of being human, our only standpoint – our voluntary participation in making right-relation among ourselves constitutes our love of God. To love humanity is to befriend God. The human act of love, befriending, making justice is our act of making God incarnate in the world.[16]

The activists show that the revolutionary hope of faith, in dethroning us from the centre of the world for the sake of what comes before us as sacred, leads to politics. Faith that turns us the right way up makes the world appear upside down; this forces a choice, either to retreat from an upside-down world or to try to change it. "I could not be leading a religious life," Gandhi wrote, "unless I identified myself with the whole of mankind, and that I could not do unless I took part in politics."[17]

Not all faith is revolutionary. The World Council of Churches has criticised much mainstream religious practice for being ossified in its certainties and for failing to honour the world-changing hopes on which faith traditions are founded:

> Either as extremely parochial or exclusively spiritual or deliberately neutral, the dominant streams of world religions have often failed to create and sustain values that uphold human interdependence and mutual responsibility in this ethos of increasing fragmentation and polarisation.[18]

Perhaps this is the sort of pragmatic religion that Marx had in mind when he criticised it as an opiate of the masses, or that Freud believed was no more than a psychological defence against the overwhelmingly threatening experience of nature. But just as we do not have to assume the same approach to religion as the bus advertisers have done, nor do we need to vindicate Marx and Freud by using faith as an analgesic. The faith reflected in John Lynes' statement and the Indian land activists' chant is hardly the sort of comfortable escape that Marx and Freud were criticising, and it would surprise both of the bus-advertising polemicists, too. Its understanding is experiential rather than notional, its consequences practical rather than theoretical, its attitude one of service rather than hubris, and its hope politically revolutionary rather than parochially self-absorbed.

Faith is the story you live in

If faith means trusting in the power that turns our lives the right way up, this extends into how we think, talk and act. The words, symbols, metaphors and practices of faith all belong to stories whose purpose is to hold and guide faithful lives and communities. Faith lives by stories. Even the rationalist view that there are no grand narratives worth believing in is a form of faith and a way of telling a story about the way the world is.

On the other hand, religious story is the thing which most seems to unsettle people with a secular worldview. For some people it is come-off-it nonsense to say that Jesus rose "on the third day" or that the Buddha attained perfect enlightenment, or that Muhammad was in frequent contact with Allah. Yet this is, I think, to forget that although a religious story may be true or false in a strict logical sense, the first question of faith is whether it is worthy of trust. A religious idea, act, story or tradition is worth putting faith in if its 'truths' are life-giving. Whether it is a fact that the Buddha Gautama was not reborn after his death matters less than whether we find the story of Buddha's nirvana meaningful and therefore worth trusting in. Similarly, we cannot know as a historical fact that Jesus rose on the third day but if in our 'prophetic imagination' he did,[19] then for us *it has happened*, whether or not it is also a historical fact.

The story we tell about the world shapes how we experience it, but stories are in turn challenged by new experience. Consider an experience of shakenness, for example. In being shaken and moved towards a more authentic way of being, my experience is of being *acted upon* and *given something*. To give this experience a home in my life I look for a story or symbol whose poetics enable me to talk about the 'givenness' of life. If my story of the world is a rationalist, secular one then I am limited to looking for rational, secular explanations for my shakenness. But my experience of shakenness is larger than an explanation of it, just as an experience of Bach's *St Matthew Passion* is more than the notes on a page.

If I happen to search Judaeo-Christian story and symbol to give a home to my shakenness I might light upon the term 'grace', meaning 'given favour' and implying a power that gives. In describing my shakenness as grace, do I imply that I am a

Christian, or that I believe God exists, or that God made the world in seven days? Not necessarily. I am merely plundering the Christian story for a meaning that can give a home to my experience of being given something by the universe. However, in beginning to use the symbols of the story I enter into its meaning and allow it to continue shaping how I experience the world. I might begin to find grace in other experiences – the passage of the seasons, for example – and to talk about them as such. As I begin to trust the story I cross a threshold into faith, albeit of a kind that neither of the bus advertisers would recognise. This is indeed the route my own journey of faith has taken. I started off as a plunderer of religious traditions because I needed their meanings to frame my experiences, and then I found their stories were taking hold of me. As the stories have become ways of seeing the world, I have felt progressively challenged and changed by them: they hold me to account.

If the story I choose (or assume) is monotheistic then I will thank God; a modern pagan might thank the Earth; or there may be some other story. At the same time, not just any story will do. For a faith story to be real, so the early Quakers believed, its truth had to be felt. As a young man George Fox knew the Bible well and lived by its stories but he felt disconnected from them until he found their truth in his own experience. His insight was that the stories did not become worthy of trust by virtue of being written in a holy book, sanctified by a holy person or inherited from holy ancestors. Nothing but a feeling for their truth in his own experience could justify investing faith in them.

The people of seventeenth-century England were thrown into the Christian story from birth and it framed the whole of existence. The founders of the Quakers and of many like-minded groups took the story as read and strove to find its meaning in their own experience of the times they were living through. Times have changed. Whilst the Bible stories still permeate our largely secular culture, most of us are bound to approach faith in a different way now that they no longer give daily experience its meaning. Rather than beginning with a given story and expecting our experience to fit into it as early Quakers did, most of us begin with our experience and look for a story by which to make sense of it. In a sense, the dissenting faith of seventeenth-century Europe was like a story looking for a world; today's largely secular society is more like a world looking for a story.

When John Lynes writes that his choice lay between the Crucified and the crucifiers, the story of the Crucifixion becomes real for him as he gazes at the arms-trade map. Similarly, Paul's road to Damascus is our road to Damascus, and ours is his. When Jesus tells his disciples, "…my peace I give you", by "you" he also means us.[20] Fox and other early Quakers claimed that when we read that Jesus rose on the third day, this means that the spirit that was in Jesus is risen in us. For the early Quakers, for John Lynes and for all those who recognise something of his experience in their own, what was happening in the ancient story is happening here, now, with us. We live the story and the story lives us, and so the solidarity of faith stretches across time.

A faith story need not prescribe a rigid view of the world. The truths of religion are fluid, evolving with the ages according to the historical circumstances in which we encounter them and to what David Ford calls the "multiple overwhelmings" of being human.[21] At the same time there is a constancy in them: although we frequently bend religious texts to our own preferences, it is their job to bend us back to their meanings by surprising and unsettling us. The Gospel of Thomas says: "Let one who seeks not stop seeking until that person finds; and upon finding, the person will be disturbed; and being disturbed, will be astounded…"[22] We read, then, not to close down experience of the world but to open it up: to be shaken, astounded and led forth.

Faith is what you do

This is Helen Steven's statement to a court in 1984, after she had entered the nuclear weapons base in Faslane in Scotland where the UK's Trident submarines are berthed:

> I am charged under an Act giving control and disposal of land to the Queen, the Lords Spiritual and Temporal, the Commons assembled in Parliament and eventually the Secretary of State. I believe the world is God's creation. This beautiful, delicate world in all its infinite wonder is threatened with extinction. That to me is blasphemy.[23]

Helen echoes the Indian activists. The "world is God's creation" and desecrating what is God's, and so comes before us in the universe, is blasphemy. While deeply personal, Helen's statement is also powerfully political; it reaches beyond the narrow *realpolitik* of Britain's security debate to call into question humanity's fundamental relationship with the universe. And when Helen's belief finds expression in action, her 'truth' becomes a political force in the world.

As Helen's action shows, holding faith with what is felt to be true re-shapes how lives are lived in such a way that the change shows up in the world. Similarly, if Indian farmers believe that the land belongs to God then this will shape how they relate to the land – in always taking care not to over-graze it, for example. Helen and the Indian activists manifest outwardly the truth they experience inwardly.

In the Judaeo-Christian tradition this embodiment of a truth is called 'testimony', after the biblical use of the term meaning a sign or proof of faith that resounds publicly in the world. Testimony in this sense means the signs, deeds, words, and lived lives of people going through the long *metanoia* of becoming faithful. The term 'testimony' is central to the Quaker tradition, binding the truths of its faith with how the community acts: it is the 'and' in Quaker faith and practice.

So testimony is not like a moral belief. Merely believing that violence is wrong, for example, is not a testimony, nor is Helen Steven's belief that the world is God's creation. Rather, Helen's testimony is the way she has put that belief into practice by trespassing on the Faslane nuclear base. Her action testifies to her holding faith with a feeling for what is true.

The Quaker peace testimony is the living-out of a conviction about what a right relationship with others means, based on a feeling for the dignity of our common being. It is made real by a determination not to violate that being and also to build the conditions in which it can flourish in the world. In honouring this, relationships are transformed, and so the peace testimony culminates in how we live and organise our communities and in social change. This is the work of the "solidarity of the shaken", moving out of life "within a lie" and towards a more authentic way of being.[24]

Just as testimony is not mere belief, nor is it mere action. The peace testimony is not the same as merely doing peace work, which is possible without any sense of faithfulness to what is sacred about life. It is quite common for a new graduate to get an internship with a peace organisation for one year and then join the staff of a think-tank advocating military expansion. When there is little or no faith to hold to in the first place, a switch like this makes sense as a savvy career move. But for someone who is trying to live out a hope for peace with the whole of their life, such a *volte-face* would feel faithless – both unethical and self-destructive. Just as a genuine smile depends on a genuine feeling of happiness, so faith-based peace work depends on a feeling for the sacredness of life, which is a constant. Testimony in this biblical sense of the term is an enduring marriage of values and action.

It is often seen as a weakness of the peace movement that perhaps most of its number are middle-aged or elderly, but the reason for this is that they are the ones still turning up. Many people I knew at university who were active for social change have more or less lost interest. Perhaps they had no over-arching narrative of what they were involved in; or they saw social change as an extra-curricular interest rather than a passion for a certain sort of life; or they lost heart when despite their best efforts the capitalist machine rolled on. In some older activists there is a powerful union of peace-making qualities:

- humane values, a deep respect for life and a natural sense of equality with others;
- the discipline of drawing on a wisdom tradition and of being repeatedly challenged in doing so;
- a commitment to community and communal learning and practice;
- an appreciation that personal, social and political challenges have a deep structure;
- patience, including a commitment to work for peace even when hopes are thin.

For these people a peace commitment is more than a political interest; it goes all the way down into who they are as human beings, expressing their feeling for what life and society are really about. Their commitment is concerned not only with stopping the next war but with the whole of life and how it is lived. This, I think, is why they keep turning up.

It is fair to say that most older peace-makers belong to a faith. Perhaps the discipline and wisdom of their faith tradition, together with its community belonging, sense of story and hope, have played a part in sustaining their commitment over the years. Some also identify themselves as being secular, demonstrating that peace-making belongs first to our humanity and can endure without 'heaven's aid' or a faith in the sacredness of life. In any case, when commitment to peace as the dignity of being goes all the way down then activists, faith-based or secular, share a more urgent and engaging purpose than arguing on the sides of buses about whether God exists.

Against a violent faith

The sceptic of religion commonly blames faith traditions for history's violence, and no wonder: the gods are not always our allies. Often, they sanction outright violence; wherever war is, there is a religious official somewhere giving it the gods' blessing. If they are not egging us on to war, the gods are accused of imposing an oppressive moralism, insisting that we are not good enough. One faith tradition says a woman must cover her skin or displease God, another that women are not good enough to be bishops, and several claim that menstruating women are unclean. In every case, the rules were written by men on behalf of their male gods. The Quaker tradition has a chequered history too: for a long time, if someone married outside the community they were disowned, for example.

This is proof enough that faith is just as good at keeping the world upside-down as turning it the right way up, but the responsibility lies not with gods but human beings. As long as we are spiritually free we are accountable for what we enthrone at the centre of our universe: 'I was only following orders from God' is no defence. The fortunes of peace through faith depend less on what religion we belong to, which is likely to be the one we are socialised into from birth, than the quality of humanity that we bring to it. The Ku Klux Klan and Martin Luther King Jr both professed the Christian faith yet practised it in irreconcilable ways. The peace-building monk Thich Nhat Hanh says he follows the teaching of the Buddha but the same claim was made by Dutthagamani, the warlord monk of old who pinned the Buddha's relics to his spear before charging into battle. What makes one right and the other wrong? We can argue that religion is only authentic insofar as it deepens our humanity but this is a judgement that only humane human beings can make, not the gods. Whilst we can choose which gods to follow, the gods are not fussy about who follows them, and so discerning 'what is God's' (and what is not) is a question of how humane our humanity, rather than how divine our gods.

For the same reason, we cannot sum up religions through history as either peaceful or violent, as oppressive or emancipatory; religions have been homes for peace-makers and war-makers, they have both oppressed and set free. Historically, we have used religion to justify wars, mobilise people to fight in them, and to cast innocents as the enemies in our story. At the same time, being religious does not cause war any more than playing football causes hooliganism. Nor does religion make peace; it can only inspire people to become peace-makers.

A word or the Word?

This chapter has imagined faith as a way of bringing meaning and passion to life and society, moving beyond the polarised question of whether we can know that God exists. But that question does not go away. A 'people of God', 'the sacred belongs to God', 'God's wisdom'… What these mean depends on what we bring to them, beginning with our own experience and a feeling for what we can honestly believe. In this, much depends on whether we read a religious text as literature or as revealing the deep structure of the universe, or both, or neither.

Read as a term of literature, 'God' might be a metaphor for whatever lies beyond the limits of our knowledge, wisdom and power. It is then a poetical way of talking about our limits and dependencies, rather than a claim that a certain deity exists. As metaphor, the language of 'God' might be a way of saying that beyond the horizon of human knowledge the universe rolls on into the distance, as in "God's wisdom is beyond our own". It might also mean that beyond our own capacity for love the universe still loves life into being. In this way, 'God' becomes a way of talking about this sense of 'beyondness'. For example, "the land is God's" might mean that the land cannot be possessed by you or me but not necessarily that there is a deity somewhere to whom it does belong.

Although most religious people would probably regard faith in a metaphorical God as being at odds with their tradition, it is still possible to read the Bible and other religious texts in this poetical way and make a case for this as authentic. Even the poet Michael Longley, who says that when it comes to the objective claims of religion he "believes nothing", still feels that life without religious language "would leave the cupboard rather bare".[25]

For others, metaphor is not enough and may be deeply unsatisfactory. Some might say that unless we appreciate that a religious text reveals the deep structure of the universe, of which God or another divine principle is the architect, we have not really grasped the meaning of the divine at all. If we think Jesus was 'just' a man, for example, rather than the one son of the creator God, then we will not appreciate the Jesus story for what it really is. According to this view, a sense of what is sacred implies that a force of divine, personal, intelligent agency is at work.

Of course there are many other ways of encountering the word 'God', and the question of whether there could be a right way is itself vexed. One way in is to read 'God-language' as metaphor and story while remaining curious about whether there is more to discover in that space of unknowing. Ben Okri said of Jesus' miracles: "It is the stories, rather than the facts, which still enchant us towards belief."[26] In the same spirit, we might approach religious text as story, and critically so, while remaining open to being "enchanted", but only, of course, if that feels an authentic thing to do. The two approaches do not sit easily together but they do exist side-by-side in the world, even in the same religious tradition.

Could we get rid of the gods altogether, even as metaphor, and still call ourselves people of faith? Some Quakers have done so, adjusting the affirmation that "there is that of God in every person" by substituting "good" for "God". This leaves very little of the kind of faith described in this chapter. In the word 'good' there is no symbol, no story, no possibility that peace is made by more than our own power alone. In particular, there is no sense of what is sacred, or that anything comes before us in the universe, and so the revolutionary implications of faith are lost.

Probably most faith-based peace-makers would say that the truths of faith are of more than metaphorical value. Many share a belief that the power which makes peace is not only within but also around us, and that even when the world seems to conspire against us as peace-makers, the universe conspires with us. After all, the power shaking us into peace-making also shakes others, and so the world. For some, this power testifies to the grace of a personal God who stands ready to work with us and through us to redeem a fallen world. For others, it is a mysterious, unnamed truth energising a commitment to peace that would otherwise quickly atrophy. Both are ways of faith. And perhaps when the 'God' of the page or the priest is elusive, we might still find its meaning in our being shaken, being turned around and, like John Lynes, being held still until we make the choice that stands up for life in a violent world.

The Buddhist activist Joanna Macy writes:

> When you look at what is happening to our world – and it is hard to look at what's happening to our water, our air, our trees, our fellow species – it becomes clear that

unless you have some roots in a spiritual practice that holds life sacred and encourages joyful communion with all your fellow beings, facing the enormous challenges ahead becomes nearly impossible.[27]

A feeling for meaning, an evolving relationship with the world, and the solidarity that this can lead into, can all help a commitment to peace to mature in a community which shares a discipline of faith. Like Joanna Macy I think we need that strength if we are to hold faith with the dignity of our common being in a meaningful way and not shrink from the hope-defying violence that pervades the world. All the same, if a peace-making commitment is sustained and deepened by faith, it nonetheless gets its grounding elsewhere: in awareness of the disturbing realities of violence. As a Falklands veteran has put it, "It's all bollocks until you're in the bang-bang."[28]

3

Facing up to violence

In 1982 Argentina and the United Kingdom fought a short, intense war for sovereignty over the Falkland Islands in the South Atlantic Ocean. The war, subsequent re-equipment and a decade of heavy defence of the islands cost Britain £4 billion, equivalent to more than £2 million for each of the 1,800 islanders at the time.[29] Almost all the Argentinian materiel, including most of the munitions, aircraft, ships, artillery and small arms, had been made in Britain, France and the United States.[30]

In the two-month war, 913 people were killed on both sides and probably three times that number were left maimed.[31] Belied by the jingoism of news headlines, the land war was a series of chaotic night-time battles fought with bayonets fixed. A large number of fighters on both sides were in their late teens; one British soldier was killed the night he turned 18.

That same night, Vince Bramley was a machine gunner in the battle of Mount Longdon. He recalls it as "combat at very close quarters, hand to hand, eye to eye, very bloody stuff", and he remembers well the scene on the top of the mountain at dawn, after the battle:

It wasn't until daylight, when I ran into the bowl on the summit and saw the number of dead people there, including my own friends and colleagues, that the shock hit me. Nobody touched me, but it was as if somebody had punched me in the stomach. And I just went into a state of shock...

I remember looking around at some of my friends who had survived as well and were in this bowl, and I hadn't realised until then that I wasn't the only one crying. And there were Argentines who had been taken prisoner, and they were crying as well. I think all of us were shocked at the extent of what we'd done to each other.[32]

Violence is what we do to each other. It is shocking because the story we tell about ourselves says that the best part of us does not want to violate life.

The word 'violence' originally meant 'break'. Just as peace means the integrity or dignity of being, violence can be understood as the breaking of it: your being, mine, ours, being itself. Although the most common definition of violence is people harming people,[33] the breaking of being is more than this. It includes those violations of life that result from oppressive social, economic and political structures, as well as harm inflicted on ecology and culture. Wherever our being is being broken, there violence is.

Yet violence is rarely random or without purpose; it functions or rather dysfunctions as an attempt to meet a need. The governments of Argentina and the United Kingdom both believed they needed to defend an exclusive right to sovereignty of the Falklands. Similarly, the rainforests are being destroyed because lumber, beef, palm oil and so on meet our needs for food, shelter, company profits, economic stability and growth. The felt need for these goods is considered more important than thinking through what a right relationship with the forest, humanity, and the Earth might mean. This means that the challenge of peace-making is not only to try to reduce and stop violence but also find ways in which fundamental needs may be met as part of a right relationship, or at least one less radically wrong.

Those who are subjected to frequent overt violence do not need its ubiquity to be pointed out. Those of us living relatively comfortable lives, virtually gated off from the daily experience of the majority world, look upon violence as if behind a window, if at all. Wealth buys distance. The artist of this book's cover image, Sarah Gittins, describes how we are caught between these realities:

The idea for *Pale Blue Window* came from two particularly vivid examples of divided experiences. One was staying on a remote Norwegian farm in the summer of 2005. The television was often on. I couldn't understand the language. But I recall the repetition of the word "Lebanon" and the images of the Lebanon war. The pictures of that terrible reality and the tranquillity of the farm could not be further removed from one another. How, I wondered, could one hold both realities in mind?

The other experience was sitting, reading a newspaper in an Edinburgh café. A place so clear in its design and calm in atmosphere that it was hard to take in the stories of conflict and environmental disaster in the pages of the newspaper. I was reminded of being in Norway. I began to imagine a series of images that I have now been working on for the past two years. These images explore ordinary events ruptured by jarring realities. In making these images I hope to bring the 'over there' into the 'here and now'.

As Sarah implies, our windows keep us in and other things out, but the world is still just there, a membrane away. What follows is an attempt to bring something of the "over there" of violence into the "here and now"; to look out from the pale blue window that separates the comforts of a privileged minority from the jarring realities of the world.

Collective violence

In the early days of its peace testimony the Quaker movement understood violence in terms of physical fighting, particularly organised warfare, and war remains perhaps the most direct and savage form of violence today. Its scale massively increased in the twentieth century with the invention of the machine gun, the bomber, the atom bomb and then the hydrogen bomb. The century saw the mass slaughter of soldiers in the First World War; the death camps, carpet-bombing, firestorms and nuclear destruction of the Second World War; a host of 'proxy wars' fought by the superpowers during the Cold War; the mass abduction of children as fighters in Cambodia and Uganda; and the machete genocide of Rwanda.

There have been over 190 armed conflicts since the Second World War.[34] In the last century 110 million people were killed in armed conflict, more than in any other century. Probably three times that number were seriously injured and 40 million people died from conflict-related famine.[35] By the 1990s over 50 million people were refugees or displaced within their own countries, most often as a direct result of armed conflict.[36]

In addition to those killed, injured and displaced, an incalculable number suffer bereavement and psychic trauma as a result of armed conflict. The most recent major study of British troops deployed to Afghanistan and/or Iraq shows that one in 15 has symptoms of Post-Traumatic Stress Disorder –

more than twice the civilian rate.[37] The risk of PTSD among soldiers appears to increase in proportion to the exposure to stressors such as killing, coming under fire, seeing people killed and picking up the dead.[38] War damages minds even more than bodies.

Despite the evident devastation of war, the ability to wage one is still a source of national pride in most nations. The five Permanent Members of the United Nations Security Council (the P5) are mandated by the UN Charter to take "primary responsibility for the maintenance of international peace and security" on behalf of the peoples of the world.[39] Yet the P5, including the UK, are also the world's most militarised states, collectively responsible for nearly two thirds of global military spending and three quarters of all arms exports.[40]

The UK has styled itself as a global leader in military power as if our collective sense of self-esteem depended on it; national pride is manifest in tanks and attack helicopters shown off at village fêtes and on school playgrounds. Perhaps the state's most cherished totem of strategic power is the Trident nuclear weapon system. One British-made nuclear warhead with an explosive yield of a million tonnes of TNT can completely destroy an area nine miles in diameter and kill everyone in it by the initial blast alone.[41] By this crude measure, the regular 48-warhead payload of one UK Trident submarine is capable of destroying most of London and the next 20 or 30 of Britain's largest cities – about 15-20 million people – instantly. Nuclear weapons may be a wildly expensive way to make the world more dangerous, as the 180 or so nuclear-weapons-free states believe, but they are also seen as a VIP ticket-to-ride with the club of world leaders. Though the UK would almost certainly not build nuclear weapons from scratch today, the hope of this post-imperial state is that Trident may yet keep the Great in Great Britain.

Personal violence

Imagine 100 randomly chosen people in Britain – roughly the number that could squeeze onto one carriage on a London Underground train. On average, according to a range of studies, we can estimate that:

+ fifteen will have been sexually abused as children. One in five girls and one in ten boys suffer sexual abuse, which is mostly repeated and typically unreported.[42] Most perpetrators are never prosecuted; in 2002 less than 300 people were convicted of the rape or attempted rape of a child;[43]

+ seven will have been seriously physically abused as children by a parent or guardian – mostly repeatedly, with babies facing the highest risks.[44] Every year around 750,000 children witness domestic violence in their homes,[45] greatly increasing the likelihood that they will have problems with violence later on as abusers and/or abused;[46]

+ thirty will have been bullied at school.[47] Worldwide, the rate of physical violence among young people doubled between 1985 and 1992;[48]

+ thirteen will have a history of self-harm as teenagers, around two thirds of them being girls;[49]

+ twenty-one will have suffered physical or sexual abuse by a partner or family member since the age of 16, and five will have experienced this at least once in the last 12 months.[50] Women in households earning under £10,000 per year are around three-and-a-half times as likely to suffer from domestic violence as those in households with incomes of £20,000 or more.[51] One in seven of the young people in the carriage will believe that abuse or violence against women is acceptable.[52]

In cases of non-sexual assault of adults outside the home, men are more likely to be the victims of violence. In all the other types of violence outlined above, the large majority of victims will be female. Victims will be concentrated among socio-economically disadvantaged people, especially those who are young. Most will not have contacted the police or medical professionals about the violence they have suffered.

In all types of violence the large majority of perpetrators will be male; most will be known to their victims, will escape accountability for their violence, and will have been victims of abuse themselves. Some of the victims in the Underground carriage will themselves be perpetrators, although others will have successfully stepped out of the cycle of violence and so broken it.

The victims of violence in the Tube carriage of 100 people will be unlikely to know that perhaps a quarter of the people there have similar, mostly untold, stories of serious violence perpetrated against them. Most of us are aware of the commonplace that British society can be violent but few will have an inkling of just how violent we are to each other.

Structured violence

Most of the world's violence against people is not the collective savagery of war, nor the interpersonal brutality in homes and on the streets, nor the self-harm that pervades society in secret – enormous though these are. Most is effected without physical aggression at all. This is the structured violence of poverty, inequality and marginalisation, by which certain groups are pushed to, or over, the very edge of society.

Like all violence, poverty and inequality are forms of broken relationship. They differ only in operating insidiously. The American prison psychiatrist James Gilligan notes that while homicides attract the lion's share of public concern about violence, social deprivation in the US accounts for a far greater mortality rate among black people than all fatalities by personal violence, black and white combined.[53] As Paul Farmer puts it, "the poor are not only more likely to suffer, they are also more likely to have their suffering silenced".[54]

The same pattern is repeated at the global level, where any one of the five biggest killer diseases – HIV/AIDS, pneumonia, dysentery, malaria and tuberculosis – has a greater health impact on individuals than all the world's war and interpersonal violence combined. These killers account collectively for a fifth of the world's entire burden of disease, affecting the poorest people by far the most.[55] The greatest risk factor for premature mortality is malnutrition, normally an indicator of extreme poverty. Worldwide, a billion people are undernourished – 15 per cent of the world's population – as part of a worsening trend that is largely due to increasing food prices and the marginalisation of people in land use.[56] Child mortality has been falling in recent years but its scale remains huge: 8.1 million children under five died in 2009, one more child in the four seconds it might have taken you to read this sentence.[57] About a third of these children die simply because of under nutrition.[58]

Once societies develop to a point where resources to meet basic physical needs are widely available, they are typically faced with another problem: inequality. The epidemiologists Richard Wilkinson and Kate Pickett have found that material inequality is closely associated with a host of social problems, such as higher levels of mistrust, mental illness, low life expectancy, child mortality, obesity, poor educational performance, teenage births, homicides, imprisonment and low social mobility.[59] Income inequality has risen substantially since the 1970s in the UK, which is one of the five most unequal countries in the world.[60] Life expectancy for a boy born today in Calton in Glasgow is 54 years; in Kensington it is 82.[61]

By poverty, stigma, the homogenisation of culture, and by policies and practices that act to divide and dominate, people may be denied the right to participate in society, to shape it, or simply to be who they are. Sometimes the dominant power aims to commandeer or colonise a marginal group, whether aggressively or paternalistically. Iain Crichton Smith, for example, described the threat to Scottish island culture as coming principally from the cultural dominance of the English language over Gaelic, which has left little room for island communities to remember who they are and to be themselves in their own home.[62] Other times the violence of marginalisation is more direct: minorities are demonised, deported or killed, as epitomised by the enormity of the Holocaust.

This violence is not merely structural but structured, in that it is inflicted as the result of choices made. When we do nothing to challenge the structured violence of our world, then we participate in its drama. We play our part at computer keyboards, the polling booth, the supermarket. The result may be a new open-cast mine in Brazil, a government that forces the unemployed to work without pay, the closure of local shops in favour of large corporations that are disconnected from the community.

Ecological violence

Eco means 'house'; our ecology is the house of all living things, made of all living things. The Earth's integrity is where peace, as right relationship, begins. If peace is imagined in terms of human relationships alone, it has a hole in its centre the shape and size of the Earth.

Since the industrial revolution, the Earth's topsoil and bio-diversity have begun to disappear and climate change has accelerated, all of which reduce the ecological carrying capacity of the planet. In the 30 years to 1991 the world lost 30 per cent of its topsoil; a complete loss would mean the end of all plant and thus animal life.[63] Human beings have now turned one half of tropical dry forests into croplands, as well as a third of temperate deciduous and Mediterranean forests and a third of grassland. The rate of species extinctions is accelerating rapidly with most major taxa in decline: an eighth of bird species, a quarter of mammals and a third of amphibians are now threatened with extinction.[64] The main driver of biodiversity loss is now climate change, although the processes that drive global warming, topsoil erosion and biodiversity loss are broadly the same: deforestation, intensive agriculture (including animal agriculture and overgrazing), industrialisation and modern commerce (including transport, power generation and building use) and consumerism (especially aviation for holidays, fossil-fuel-based personal transport and leisure shopping).[65] Ecological violence comes down to how we are living and organising our societies.

Without carbon mitigation policies in place, by the 2070s global temperatures are likely to be 4°C above pre-industrial levels, according to the current estimate by the Meteorological Office.[66] At this level entire regions would begin to see major declines in crop yields; there would be a dramatic increase in famine, possibly a billion people suffering water shortages, and extreme weather events, floods and fires.[67] The Amazon rainforest along with other large ecosystems could collapse, leading to between a fifth and a half of all species facing extinction.[68] Tens to hundreds of millions of people would be affected by flooding; malnutrition, heat stress and diseases such as malaria and cholera would increase; possibly 200 million people would be displaced.[69] There would also be positive feedback leading to accelerated change in the climate.[70]

In Britain we still produce an average of 11.5 tonnes of greenhouse gases per person per year, of which 4.5 tonnes are due to choices within our direct control. Most of these emissions are due to car use, aviation (including air-freighted goods), eating meat and dairy products, heating and powering homes and buying new stuff, especially clothes and imported gadgets.[71] An ecologically informed commitment to peace is at odds with these choices. How could we not now see them as chosen acts of ecological and, in turn, of social violence? Two decades after 'global warming' entered the popular lexicon we have barely begun to take climate change seriously in Britain. Although a culture of concern seems to be developing we are still half-asleep. We need to wake up, for the house is on fire.

To keep the global temperature rise within 2°C above pre-industrial levels, the Intergovernmental Panel on Climate Change says that it would cost the world no more than three per cent of Gross Domestic Product between now and 2030.[72] This global bill, just under $1,800 billion per year, is in the same order as current military expenditure.[73] The urgency is extreme: global carbon emissions must peak no later than 2015 to keep within the IPCC limit, and even this could still put Bangladesh under water.[74]

According to the Heinrich Böll Stiftung, for poorer countries to slow their increase in carbon emissions while still meeting fundamental needs, richer countries would need to shoulder the larger burden of the response. The Stiftung estimates that the European Union's share of the annual $1,800bn cost would be 22.6 per cent,[75] or 3.7 per cent for the UK.[76] This is a very large sum, equivalent to £42bn in the UK, but still less than the £47bn we devote to buying new clothes and shoes each year and the £45bn we spend on all goods over the six-week Christmas period.[77] Why are scarce resources squandered in this way? Partly, at least, because the viability of the economic system depends on continued growth, which means that industrialised societies are structured around continued consumer spending.

Our ecological emergency shows how carbon emissions anywhere affect life everywhere, how biodiversity loss, topsoil loss and climate change all reinforce each other, and how we are dependent on the Earth because it gives rise to our life and sustains it. Therefore, perhaps more clearly than any other problem the world has faced, the climate crisis demonstrates that in our universe all things are interwoven. It shows, as clearly as anything ever could, that we are the neighbourhood and it is us, so there really is something other than us at the centre of our universe. In this light, the crisis of climate change calls us not only to rebuild our lives and societies around a low-carbon economy. It also calls us to question our fundamental relation with the world, for the cause of the crisis is not a lack of energy-saving light bulbs but a broken relationship with the Earth, in which we see ourselves as coming first.

Our presumption of entitlement to the Earth as a commodity is a colossal mistake; it is as if industrial society is burning down the house it lives in and calling it prudent economics. The ecological consequences threaten catastrophe to millions of people, to millions of species and to the long-term capacity of the Earth to sustain diverse life. It is a global emergency.

System of violence

Collective, personal, structured and ecological violence belong to the same nexus. The military is a massive contributor to global warming – the UK armed forces account for one per cent of our greenhouse gas emissions, equivalent to the entire output of Senegal.[78] Conversely, climate change will cause increasing global instability, and most nations are likely to respond by ramping up military spending. Massive military investment worldwide diverts attention and resources away from tackling poverty and injustice, which in turn creates the conditions for personal and collective violence. All these and countless other associations show that the many forms of violence all belong to the same system of suffering and broken relationships.

Gandhi wrote that when violent interventions are thought to 'work', we become more prepared to resort to them to solve problems in the future.[79] But are there not forms of violence that only violence in turn can stop? While admiring Gandhi, his biographer Bhikhu Parekh criticised him for failing to recognise that:

> violence need not be accompanied by hatred and ill-will or be uncontrolled. Like non-violence it too can be restrained, measured, born out of love for both the victims and the perpetrators of injustice, and used to arrest human degradation.[80]

If Gandhi were still around to respond, he might say that in supporting one form of violence – even those violations that are ostensibly ethically constrained – you support them all.

Consider armed peace-keeping. Although it can stop bloodshed and help to create space for peace processes, its effectiveness depends on the threat and use of violence; that is why it is *armed*. What are the implications of this? First, armed peace-keeping requires everything that the armed forces need in order to function, including a mainstream social culture supporting military intervention abroad and describing war as more heroic than horrific. Support armed peace-keeping and you support recruiting young people into the armed forces and training them to kill, with all the personal and social implications that involves. Effective recruitment advertising glamorises the armed forces and obscures the horrors and terrors of war; a more honest approach would not attract enough recruits. Recruitment depends also on a pool of young people from disadvantaged backgrounds, as relatively few well-off youngsters enlist.

Support for armed peace-keeping similarly implies acceptance of the research and manufacture of arms which, in a globalised world where no one country manufactures all its own military equipment, means supporting an international arms trade. This trade is economically unviable without government subsidy and, as there are not enough human rights-loving, non-bellicose, democratically accountable states to buy our arms, we sell them to corrupt regimes. Support armed peace-keeping and we have to support its consequences: soldiers with post-traumatic stress or without homes after leaving the forces, university departments designing guns instead of renewable technologies, a world awash with weapons, a huge carbon footprint, and myriad other unseen consequences rolling outwards across the world and onwards into the future. Whether or not we think armed peace-keepers are sometimes necessary – and there are usually non-violent alternatives[81] – its implications are not as "restrained, measured, born out of love" as the initial impulse to deploy them might have been.

This does not get us off the hook of the very difficult dilemmas involved in refusing to use violence to stop it. I think we do have to accept that even if there are always non-violent ways of transforming violence, we will not necessarily know what they are. If we do, we might yet fall short of the commitment they require of us as individuals and as societies; the nations are practised in war-making but still novices at best, as are we all, when it comes to peace-making.

At the same time, because violence is a tangle of structures, processes, culture and behaviour, the will to violate in order to stop violence always feeds it in some way. It pushes away the possibility of making ploughshares out of swords; in this sense it always fails even when it seems to work. And no-one has to be a pacifist to recognise the horrors that violence, even when self-justified as humanitarian, can lead us into. The torture at Abu Ghraib jail in Iraq shocks but should not surprise; it is there in every war.

Other than to the shareholders and others who profit from the military industries and trade, it cannot make sense for the world to spend over \$1,500 billion every year on preparing for war.[82] If we want peace then we should prepare for peace. Political and financial capital would be better spent, and jobs would be better found, investing in preventing violent conflict before the question of a 'last resort' armed intervention arises. Similarly, we could invest more heavily in supporting abused young people to break the cycle of violence before they offend in turn, in place of building more and more prisons to hold them in when they do. And we are better off focusing resources on how to stop the Amazon rainforest collapsing than waiting for it to happen. This is not the stuff of ideology but the pragmatism of common sense.

There is good news in all this, too. Violence pervades the world but does not define it. Create space for peace to flourish and it is more difficult for violence to take it over. Undermine one form of violence, or one stage in a process of violence, and the entire nexus is confronted. Every child who learns to handle conflict well in the playground is helping in a small way to abolish war. No kind of violence is inevitable and all can be transformed given the will, imagination, commitment and solidarity. But for that, we have to ask how violence arises and why there is so much of it.

4

Understanding violence

There is no commonly agreed understanding of the causes of violence. In the case of youth violence, for example, the World Health Organisation discusses some 46 significant risk factors, from difficulties during birth to consumerism.[83] This complexity notwithstanding, two claims are worth making. First, violence is the consequence of certain choices made: cycles of violence can be intensified or broken by making choices. Second, violence is strongly conditioned by the situations and systems in which it occurs. This means that by influencing the context in certain ways, the extent of violence can be increased or decreased, although not always predictably.

We are not born violent. According to the WHO, "...while biological and other individual factors explain some of the predisposition to aggression, more often these factors interact with family, community, cultural and other external factors to create a situation where violence is likely to occur."[84] Yet these risk factors alone do not show how they relate together within the systems of which they are a part. We cannot say, for example, that since high unemployment levels tend to correlate with high levels of physical violence among young people, unemployment causes violence. We cannot define with confidence the social and psychological pathway by which unemployment impinges on behaviour. How we understand the association of unemployment with violence has much to do with the story we tell about how violence arises: is it a competition for limited resources, or an attempt to escape oppression? Is it connected with shame? Or is unemployment associated with something else, such as poverty, that itself generates conditions of violence in some other way?

These questions have no simple answers but by recognising violence in terms of a process – that is, as part of a system of relationships, culture and social structures – some sense can be made of why it happens. Below is an attempt to summarise some useful ways of talking about violence. None of the ideas here can fully account for violence, and most are overlapping and mutually reinforcing.

Violence of the cornered

First, violence can be a rational choice, which is not to say an effective or moral one; it can be a way of surviving when other options seem unavailable.

Alternatives to Violence Project (AVP) workshops are intensive group sessions that help people to handle conflict and violence. Many people who attend say they need to deal with their anger, often labelling themselves 'angry people' as if they ought to be ashamed of how they feel. The word 'anger' is based on the Indo-European root *ang*, meaning 'strangulation' (where it also appears). Curiously, if you try saying *ang* and stop on the g you'll find that after a while you can't breathe; if you were stuck like this for long enough you would probably involuntarily start to lash out in order to release yourself. Anger is like this – it is the energy that charges an attempt to break free of oppression, whether actual or perceived.

Often AVP workshop participants say they have committed violent acts because they have felt cornered (i.e. metaphorically strangled), for example by a shaming comment made to them. Unable to articulate an effective, assertive response, violence has seemed the only way to escape crushing humiliation. In such cases there has often been a strong will not to be violent but the immediate felt need to escape a shaming situation has exploded in brutal reaction. A person 'flips', 'sees red', 'goes blank', 'loses it', and may feel confusion, regret and self hate afterwards. The prison psychiatrist James Gilligan writes:

> The purpose of violence is to diminish the intensity of shame and replace it as far as possible with its opposite, pride, thus preventing the individual from being overwhelmed by the feeling of shame.[85]

Camila Batmanghelidjh founded the young people's support service, Kids Company, in south London. Like James Gilligan, she appeals to us to recognise that violence is a rational adaptation from the point of view of a resourceful young person struggling to survive repeated abuse.[86] Many young people see violent behaviours as the only way to obtain what they need to endure their environment and recover lost power and dignity. These are genuine needs and as long as violence appears to be the only viable way to meet them, it would be irrational to give it up. For the cornered, both violence and their attempts to overcome it are part of a struggle. The challenge of peace-making is to wage that struggle so that needs may be effectively met without violence.

Young people at centres like Kids Company face not only the immediate violence of an abusive parent or dangerous neighbourhood, but also the economic and political structures that create such cornering conditions in the first place. The logical consequence of the political-economic status quo is billionaires and paupers; it could not be otherwise in a system driven by a competative profit motive. This creates a majority underclass, oppressed and cornered by the complacent minority wealth of those above it. The result, seen on the streets of south London, Los Angeles, São Paulo, Gaza, is not only the structured violence of poverty, inequality and marginalisation. It is also the personal and collective violence that these conditions engender as an apparently rational stratagem for survival. The consequence is widespread violent struggle and a criminal justice system bursting at the seams. "You cannot work for one day with the violent people who fill our prisons and mental hospitals for the criminally insane," writes James Gilligan, "without being forcibly and constantly reminded of the extreme poverty and discrimination that characterize their lives."[87]

The violence of the dominant political and economic system is like dark matter in physics, writes Slavoj Žižek: it "may be invisible, but it has to be taken into account if one is to make sense of what otherwise seem to be 'irrational' explosions of subjective violence".[88] For this reason, nonviolence movements are not only concerned with refusing to allow oppression to corner them into violence, but with overcoming oppression itself.

The powerful get cornered too. *War and Peace* is a story of wealthy, influential families whose power is eclipsed almost entirely by political and social forces way beyond their immediate influence. Tolstoy ends his epic with an essay, in which he argues that history has momentum and direction of its own that corners even the most powerful leaders into certain courses of action. The essence of Tolstoy's argument is that as historical events gather momentum, the options imagined as possible become progressively fewer:

> All the impossible commands are inconsistent with the course of events and do not get carried out. Only the possible ones link up into a consecutive series of commands corresponding to a series of events, and are carried out.[89]

John Nott, Defence Secretary at the time of the Falklands War, would perhaps recognise this. Looking back, he wrote: "In politics … you can't decide events: they take control of you. You get carried away with the emergency of the situation that confronts you."[90] In the run-up to the second Iraq war the decision to invade was made long before people took to the streets to protest. Years earlier political leaders had set in motion a chain of events – diplomatic, military, economic, political – that became increasingly irreversible as they proceeded. The massive demonstrations on 15 February 2003 took place long after the movement towards war had gathered an almost unstoppable momentum. Do these examples vindicate Tolstoy's view? Not entirely. It is making excuses, or what Jean-Paul Sartre called "bad faith", to think that violence is inevitable; for there are always choices to be made, however narrow the options appear to be.

Violence of the violated

Heinz Reinheimer, the son of a print shop owner in 1930s Germany, recalled later how most of his neighbours projected their hopes onto Hitler as a saviour figure:

> I saw how, particularly in bourgeois circles, particularly among the middle classes, hope was placed on this man Hitler, who had indeed promised to lead Germany to a new position of respect. In short, he would deliver us from all the evils that had befallen us… It seemed to be the only hope at that time, in the middle of a world which knew nothing but emergency decrees, unemployment, despair.[91]

Reinheimer's allusions are to the desperate state of German society between the wars. After the First World War, Germany had been punished with loss of territory, a levy to compensate the Allies for the war, emasculation of its armed forces, and an enforced formal acceptance of the blame for causing the war. To the Allies this seemed fair reparation for the havoc caused by the war and a reasonable precaution against a resurgent, bellicose Germany. Indeed, many people in Britain and France accused their governments of being too soft. The policy's effects, when combined with the Great Depression, were ruinous for the German people, leading to hyper-inflation, mass unemployment and social unrest. They saw the Allies as acting vengefully to violate their German national dignity and drive a proud people into the ground. This is why, according to Reinheimer, so many people invested their hopes in Hitler's promise of national renewal.

This does not imply that the Allied Powers brought the war on themselves, as if Hitler's choice to invade Poland played no part. Rather, it is to say that the war's genesis was part of a complex process that began much earlier than 1939, and that the sense of violation and resentment felt by the German people played a significant role. In this light, the Second World War, like all wars, was part of a repeating cycle of violence.

We find the same cycle operating in homes and neighbour-hoods. Camila Batmanghelidjh again:

> We talk of terrorism and the threats of violence perpetrated by extremists and fundamentalists. Yet it is my view that the greatest terrorism lurks behind closed doors. It is the terrorization of children who then grow to terrorize in revenge.[92]

The radical Brazilian educationist Paulo Freire called this violence among the oppressed "horizontal", in contrast with 'vertical', revolutionary violence against the oppressor.[93] He believed that people who are oppressed by social structures often internalise and incarnate the values of their own oppression; that is, they accept their oppression uncritically and deflect the misery onto their peers.

Perhaps a similar process was at work among those incarcerated in Nazi concentration camps, where newcomers were victimised as part of the survival strategy of those who had achieved seniority, according to Primo Levi who witnessed this first-hand. What Levi described as the camp's total "state of coercion",[94] and the apparent impossibility of revolutionary violence (or nonviolence) against their gaolers, meant that violence directed between peers became inevitable.

Because it operates cyclically, violence cannot be understood in terms of its acts alone; it is also a process that conditions how we act. When a parent abuses a child or one country invades another, the conditions of future violence are generated. The traumatised child is put at risk of becoming a terrorising young person; the violence in Iraq rages on long after "mission accomplished" is proclaimed. Violence rarely, perhaps never, solves a problem without creating another.

By refusing to allow past violations to determine our present and future choices, cycles of violence can be broken. Each choice aimed at stepping out of the cycle, whether successful or not, is a peace act. If we want to prevent the next war but one, we should not begin the next war. If we want to prevent domestic abuse in the next generation, we should love well the children of this generation before they become parents.

For an abused and now violent child, writes Camila Batmanghelidjh, "[the] only thing which can return them from the abyss is the capacity to rekindle their ability to feel, by feeling for them."[95] This solidarity, when it is courageous enough to face the child's own violent behaviour, can support them to recognise new, more life-affirming choices and lead with hope to a less violent, less violated life.

So, peace also runs in cycles. The relationship between parent and child is perhaps the most important in the world. Nothing facilitates peace more deeply or powerfully than when parenting is founded on love – love of self and love of the child. This not only facilitates the child's growth but also supports the child to create the right relationships of peace as he or she grows into adulthood. As parents, and as the corporate parent that is society, we do not need to love perfectly but we do need to love enough.

Violence as norm

In the 1960s, Stanley Milgram conducted his so-called Abraham Experiments. In these, the experimenter persuaded volunteers to administer apparently real (but actually fake) electric shocks to another person (actually an actor). As the experiment progressed, the volunteer was expected to administer increasingly intense shocks on a scale labelled from "Slight Shock" to "Danger: Severe Shock". If a volunteer desisted, the experimenter repeated the same line: "The experiment requires that you go on."

In many cases, voltages reached nominally lethal levels, despite the actor's increasingly desperate pleas. Why did so many volunteers readily comply with the violence of the experiment? Milgram speculated that volunteers felt they ought to "fit into the structure of the experimenter", who by his authority made the electric shocks an acceptable norm. Milgram also speculated that the sheep-like behaviour of the volunteers might account for public complicity in large-scale violence such as warfare.[96]

A further way of understanding violence, then, is in looking for how it has become normalised and thus legitimised, so that we participate in it unthinkingly. When violence is broadly normative in a certain social context, non-violent choices are more difficult to make. This means that when everyone around a subject (where a 'subject' might mean a person, group, community, etc.) is committing acts of violence, it becomes socially abnormal for that subject to act non-violently.

Consider this man describing a recent bayonet battle against Japanese soldiers during the Second World War, and clipped from the *Herald Tribune* by co-founder of the radical Catholic Worker movement Dorothy Day:

> [My father] should have been with us and seen how good it was. We got into them good and proper, and I can't say I remember much about it, except that it made me feel pretty good. I reckon that was the way with the rest of the company, by the way my pals were yelling all the time.[97]

One young man drives a bayonet through the body of another. Their fathers wait at home, one in America, one in Japan, worried for their sons. One is glad to see his son home and proud of his victory, the other buries his son or never sees his body again. Judged with a cooler head and away from the white heat of battle, the scene would horrify anyone but the soldier says he feels "pretty good". "Is this a Christian speaking?" wonders Dorothy Day.

But we do not know this soldier. It is possible that he has no morals we could recognise as 'Christian' but the truth is likely to be more shocking: that he is a common man with an ordinary sense of right and wrong who has been shaped into a killer. His admission that he cannot remember details could be a symptom of hidden, as yet unacknowledged trauma; we do not know. We might nonetheless imagine how important it would be for him to believe, for as long as he possibly could, that what he did was right. We might also try to understand that by the rules of the brutally re-ordered world of war, his action was normal, legitimate, necessary.

Almost certainly none of these men, faced with the inhumanity of the prospect of killing, laid down his weapon, so we should not expect this one soldier to be the black sheep. That would be to follow the rules of another world, outside war, where people are expected to think for themselves about their choices in full conscience. In his case, the violence of battle has everyone caught up in it, as if the war itself were doing all the thinking. It has become the normal state of affairs, legitimising what in a civilian context we would call murder, and "the experiment requires that you go on". War has its own rules and this soldier, like his comrades, cannot think outside of them, does not wish to, possibly could not bear to.

The normalisation of violence is a necessary condition for the armed forces to function. Behind all the glossy recruitment advertising their purpose is a coarse one, as General Sir Michael Rose reminds us: "[No] other group in society is required either to kill other human beings, or expressly sacrifice themselves for the nation."[98] For the armed forces to be what they are, the will to harm and kill others must not only be normalised but normative, and a great deal of time and money is spent training young recruits to overcome their inhibition to killing. David Grossman, a retired US military officer, trains new soldiers to achieve exactly this:

> [Inside] most healthy human beings is this powerful resistance to killing your own kind… [T]his physiological phenomenon can be dealt with in several ways. One is to… remain calm, cool, calculating in the heat of battle, and we're doing that [in the training programme]. The other thing is to have a condition reflex in place so that even at the moment of truth, the shot's there [*snaps fingers*] and you fire without conscious thought.[99]

If Grossman is right then the soldier's first enemy is his own second thoughts about killing. But soldiers are not unthinking people, and after the fighting those repressed second thoughts can surface. It becomes, as Vince Bramley said, shocking to remember what has been done, and then the nightmares begin.

Just as shocking is that ordinary folk can be made capable of such extraordinary violence, and that in Britain this begins with people as young as 16; the state trains the young to kill before they are considered mature enough to vote, drink, smoke or watch an adult film. At 18 they may be sent to fight in wars chosen by their parents' generation, and by then the law will have locked them into the forces until they are 22. The entire project is framed in heroic terms, thereby creating a legitimating story for it, and is wrapped in promises of adventure and a sense of purpose. It is targeted at young people with the fewest life options in the most disadvantaged neighbourhoods, long before they even reach recruitment age. As a former soldier told me, by the time a teenager has reached the door of the army recruiting office he has already been recruited.

Martie Rafferty, a Quaker who has worked extensively with traumatised soldiers, observes that we all create the warrior,[100] and we are all involved in the unthinkingness that silently legitimises their violence. Taxi-drivers advertise arms export companies on their cabs, parents yell at or smack their children on the way to the shops. We inflict ecological violence by eating meat and dairy or flying for holidays to France just because that's what you do, and the experiment requires that you go on.

Whether violence is normalised or abnormalised depends on the story we choose to tell ourselves about the world we are in. If our language and culture are oppressive, generate hatred or indifference or marginalise life-giving possibilities, then we will reflect this symbolic violence in how we live. A society that glorifies war will be in one before long.

The theologian Walter Wink argues that close to the heart of our social culture is a story that violence can make good.[101] This "myth of redemptive violence" is widely normative and deeply influential in our appetite for self-justified violations, he argues, from petty vengefulness aimed at 'teaching someone a lesson' to nuclear retaliation. If the war in Afghanistan is described heroically as a way of freeing women from the patriarchal violence of the Taliban, then we are more willing to accept carpet-bombing and water-boarding as being all in a good cause.

A commitment to peace entails making sure that the violence of our environment does not determine who we are and what we do. It means challenging violence that is so normalised in society as to be almost beyond notice. It also means repeatedly rediscovering who and what we really are as humane beings. For those of us for whom peace is a commitment of faith, it means holding a feeling for what is sacred in the integrity of our being, so that we may make peace-making choices even in violence-making conditions. All this means keeping faith with what life is really about for us – with a sense of what matters most – such that violence may not so easily sweep us along and make us feel "pretty good", as it did that American soldier with his bloodied bayonet.

Violence of rivals

Just about the most popular item of Quaker merchandise is a printed tea-towel entitled *The Two Mules: A Fable for the Nations*. Two cartoon mules, each with its own pile of hay set apart, are tied together. As each goes for its hay, the rope pulls taut and the mules strain against each other. When this fails, question marks appear above their heads. Then comes the *eureka!* moment: the mules move together to the first pile of hay and eat, then to the second.

Before they choose to cooperate, the mules' rivalry symbolises a basic condition of humanity: we need to meet our needs and want to meet our wants, yet are constrained by others trying to do the same. If cooperation *in* power is not immediately possible, or not wanted, then a contest *for* power is inevitable. If that contest is based on subjugating or destroying rivals then it becomes violent. This violence finds many petty forms, such as the pitched mêlée of shoppers' elbows as they pour into Selfridges when the sales open, or the defence of gang territories. It is there, too, in bloody conflicts for access to scarce natural resources such as oil, water, diamonds, and fertile land.

When the struggle is not merely for access but for control, the violence of rivals becomes more sinister. In the Cold War arms race the superpowers expended vast sums and fought numerous proxy wars for the sake of gaining some advantage over each other, while their absurd drama took the world to the brink of nuclear annihilation. One honest motivation was to minimise the vulnerability that each superpower felt in the face of the other; a more sinister one was to control the future of the world. The pathological aim of each protagonist was to have everything and fear nothing. At stake was the power not only to participate in the game, or even to dominate it, but to control the whole playing field.

Depending on our position on that field, we might be trying to escape another's control, gain control, or maintain control over others. If I am weaker I seize power from you to survive; if we are peers I seize power from you to stay ahead of the game; if I am stronger I seize power to achieve supremacy over all potential rivals. This is the 'game' that certain nations are playing out in each region of the world and globally. When a state projects power abroad it typically describes this in terms of national security or humanitarian goals, but the primary purpose is often to protect or advance its place in the international pecking order. We must take account of this if we are to understand Britain's current nuclear weapons policy, for example, as well as the UK's military interventions in recent years.

This game of *realpolitik* is based on an assumption: that we are all rivals competing for a finite power or resource. Vulnerability in the face of rivals is to be minimised and even eliminated, rather than accepted as an inevitable and humanising part of the human condition. Because of the felt need to reduce vulnerability as far as possible, accumulating a fair share of power is not enough; each player will try to get as much as it can. A business is never quite big enough until it is the biggest (although then, paradoxically, the paranoia intensifies). Rivals are condemned to a game of empire-building that no-one can win, or not for long. The limitless accumulation of power is unsustainable; sooner or later all empires fall, usually by the same means by which they arose: violence.

Coveting greater power of control means one thing for the already-powerful, but for those whose power to shape society has been stolen from them, it means quite another. Dictators try to eliminate all resistance to their supremacy; Western democracies manage dissent in order to confine it to the margins. This oppression can provoke violent responses from the disenfranchised, either vertically against the powerful or horizontally among the oppressed.

If power begins to leech away from the dominant forces, their fear intensifies, leading to violent attempts to regain full control. We see this in crowd-control tactics that become more brutal in proportion not to the actual threat from the crowd, but to police commanders' perceived loss of control. Similarly, Hannah Arendt noted a rise in brutality in British colonies as the Empire wound down and again when the Soviet Union was struggling to control vassal states like Czechoslovakia. "Rule by sheer violence," she wrote, "comes into play where power is being lost."[102]

We also find this in the attempt particularly by Western powers to control other states in order to suppress any potential threats to their global dominance. The aim is to preserve the West as a gated community of privilege in a violent global neighbourhood of injustice, suffering and resentment; therefore the struggle for resources for defending the gates against those on the outside eclipses efforts to right the wrongs they have suffered. The international security expert Paul Rogers labels this strategy "liddism": keeping the lid on a world boiling with resentments.[103] Similarly, Diana Francis contrasts "pacification", being the attempt to subjugate a potentially threatening other, with "peacebuilding", which sees every person and community as deserving of justice in a shared peace.[104] "Liddism" and "pacification" are as precarious as empire-building, and indeed amount to much the same thing. Yet they are preferred because their alternative – justice – calls the presumption of Western dominance into question. As the pressures brought by climate change mount, the West will find it more difficult to keep the lid on the rest of the world, probably leading to the increasing use of 'pacifying', top-down violence.

The violence of rivals leaves little room for the possibility that power can be used cooperatively to meet common needs. For the political philosopher Thomas Hobbes, however, this kind of violent competition was an inevitable fact of the "brutish" character of human nature:

> And therefore if any two men desire the same thing, which nevertheless they cannot both enjoy, they become enemies [and] … endeavour to destroy or subdue one another.[105]

Marx was not much more hopeful. He described competition between rivals as the necessary means by which we overthrow history's procession of contradictions and drive the engine of progress, one bloody battle after another.

The early Quaker William Penn understood violence in a similar way: "There appears to me but three things upon which peace is broken, viz., to keep, to recover, or to add."[106] Penn, however, was more optimistic about humanity. He believed that a society structured on cooperation, which could be framed by a commitment to justice, fundamental freedoms and equitable distribution of power, would facilitate the nobler side of humanity.

In its way, the world we have created vindicates all three thinkers, including the hopefulness of William Penn. We are likely to identify our neighbour as a rival when there is little trust, reciprocity, mutuality, sense of commonality or respect for others' dignity; to this extent Hobbes' chilling indictment of humanity holds true. But this is not how we start out in conditions that are more conducive to peace. In daily life, conflicts pop up all the time but so does cooperation; we have to cooperate with others just to occupy the same pavement (it would just be too exhausting to try to push everyone else out of the way). Sometimes cooperation is inappropriate: for example, if we cooperate unconditionally with the political-economic system, we facilitate its violence. When cooperation is based on justice, however, it is always part of the peace, for peace implies shared power.

The message of the *Two Mules* cartoon is that cooperation is simply a better choice than violence: it not only means that everyone gets what they need, but it also turns rivals into comrades. But for me it makes its point too easily: if only we were nice to each other, it seems to imply, the world would be a better place. For me, and I know many Quakers feel the same way, peace is a passion leading into all manner of creative conflicts that disturb the status quo and shake us up in the process. The universe of the two mules seems to bypass all this. One day I asked a Quaker colleague, "Why doesn't one mule just kill the other and have done with it?" "Because it'd be tied to a dead mule," he shot back. Now that's a tea-towel with a message.

Violence of hubris

'No dogs or Bantu'

> Common sign on whites-only beaches,
> apartheid South Africa

'It is easier to educate a dog than a Roma child.'

> Italian politician, 2011[107]

'I like it when a woman has ambition. It's like seeing a
dog wearing clothes.'

> Joke on US TV show, 2010[108]

When we exalt ourselves above others, violence ensues. As
soon as we see our neighbour as a dog, we pave the way for
treating them as such, or worse. This is the essence of hubris: a
self-justified, even self-righteous, sense of entitlement to violate
others, which can lead to barbaric forms of violence. Black South
Africans are forced from their homes and into ghettos, Roma,
Jews, and homosexuals are rounded up for the gas chambers, and
women are beaten in their own homes.

The early Quakers believed that this kind of prideful violence
belonged to the 'lusts', meaning something like ego-cravings or
false desires. Following the fourth chapter of the Letter of James,
they believed that such cravings put our own egos at the centre
of the world and led us into violence and war. Even when that
violence is for noble ends, the sense of entitlement to violate
others is still self-justified hubris: it belongs with the lusts.

The Quaker activist and poet Alastair McIntosh writes:

> We forget that hubris, which is a state that we accept
> almost as a norm in our helter-skelter hustle and bustle
> society, is a word that has its origin in the Greek *hybris*,
> meaning "wanton violence".[109]

We can at least partly understand the Crusades as violence of the
proud, and George W. Bush would have us include as a crusade the
current US-led war in Afghanistan.[110] Pride also suffuses fantasies
of social or ethnic purity that can lead dominant elites to purge
society of groups in weaker positions. The ambitions of European
empires, in all their colonial institutions from paternalistic 'help'
for the poor through to the slave trade, have presumed white
superiority. Pride is in play when a parent presumes a right to hurt
their child, a city trader tells a beggar to get a job, or industrialised
society commodifies the Earth. It is there in the army NCO who
says: "If I'm bollocking [a female] and I say they've got saggy tits
that's nothing to do with sexual harassment that is me bollocking
them the same I do with any bloke."[111]

The violence of marginalisation seems to diminish when we
start to find differences more interesting than threatening. The
time has gone, at least in most parts of the world, when it was
normative to imagine women as witches, or black people as
slaves, or Jewish and Roma people as *Untermenschen* in order
to legitimate, in each case, public-approved violence. Even so, a
woman can still be abused with impunity just because she is a
woman, a black man can be victimised by the state just because
he is black, and as I write Roma settlers are being evicted from
France just because they are Roma.

Every society has its history of pushing their unwanted to its
margins and its own idiom for legitimating it: in Serbo-Croat it is
čišćenje, in French it is *épuration*, in English it is clearances. Only

the Russian *pogrom* avoids euphemism, meaning 'thunderous devastation'; the rest are all terms meaning to clean or purify. Each is a nexus of policies shaping cultural values, economic systems and political organisation in ways that effect and legitimate violence against socially vulnerable groups. But this kind of violence begins more insidiously; before the beatings there is the banter: "Have you heard the one about the dog that wore clothes?"

We cannot presume ourselves to be superior to others, or to the Earth, without stepping outside the sense of mutual belonging that is the very essence of a commitment to peace. Peace, as the dignity of our being, has no place for the conceit that there are others who deserve to be treated like dogs, enemies to kill, an Earth to plunder. It is never ours to cast out our neighbour, as the South African theologian, Ananias Mpunzi, wrote:

> It is not enough to say that we are persons in our uniqueness, however vital it is to say that. We are persons in the unity that holds people in the powerful give-and-take of love and acceptance... We must shout loud and clear and far and wide to anyone who will hear: "You are persons made for love. Don't cut yourself off from that love by thinking and acting as if you were superior to anyone else, and especially by acting as if you were inferior to anyone else."[112]

Violence as symptom

If any of the foregoing ideas are useful, it is not as straight explanations of violence but as filters to help bring certain of its characteristics in clearer view. Violence itself is not comprehensible (literally 'able to be contained'); its reality exceeds understanding, and however much we think we understand there is always more to know. Furthermore, it is not all as ill-motivated as I have suggested in this chapter; love is often involved even as part of a violent act. In the eighteenth century, many poor women, afraid they could not care for their new-born, left them at the steps of the Coram Hospital in London to grow up as orphans in care. They would cut a coin in two and leave half with the child and keep the other half themselves in hope of one day being reunited. The coins are now on display at the Coram Museum, symbolising both the rupture of relationship and a loving hope: a tangle of violence and love beyond the judgement of a later century.

Violence is noisy; in breaking our being it confuses our being. The overwhelming complexities of violence notwithstanding, if we take all the ideas described here together, they reveal two things that are vital for informing a commitment to peace. The first is that violence is a symptom of relationships that have gone wrong between individuals, communities, states; with ourselves; with the Earth, and that these conditions are structured by the injustices and oppression of societies.

Second, the world is violent because we have made it so; or rather, we have yet to make it otherwise. Collectively we have yet to make the life-giving choices that break cycles of violence and build the conditions of peace in which such choices are more possible. That world is one in which fewer people feel cornered by their situation, fewer are violated, fewer see violence as normal, fewer believe it is a dog-eat-dog world, and fewer are lost in their own hubris.

This is why our common peace-making challenge as individuals, communities and nations is to create the vibrancy and justice of right relationship in every part of life and society. The practice of peace concerns how we relate to each other, to society and to our ecological context, and how we work for social change. This is more than a passive, ideological pacifism that stands up to condemn violence and then sits down again. It must also mean more than abstaining from physically violent behaviour, important though that is. It means making and encouraging choices that belong to the full dignity and aliveness of our shared being. This promise of humanity waits to be realised in every choice we make; it is what our lives and societies can be about. Our task is not to achieve total change by our own efforts; that would perhaps be a form of hubris in itself; it is, as the Quaker Joyce Pickard once said, to pray that we may play some part in this work of peace.[113]

A commitment to peace flows from who and what we are, and from what we are becoming. For such a commitment to take root it matters how alive and free we are. It is hard to imagine how we could even begin to do this without a feeling for what is sacred in life, without a sense of what matters most, without each other, and without a narrative of hope that supports us to hold faith. In other words, our common vocation as peace-makers flows from – and only from – becoming more fully human, and in turn it brings us more fully into life. Yet if Martians landed in our homes in Britain they would be likely to find us watching TV; in our communities, shopping; and at work, performing machine-like jobs for authoritarian businesses. We are in large part estranged or alienated from who and what we truly are by the social structures we participate in, lost in what we are not. Peace-making is next-to-impossible without beginning first to recover who we are, often despite the norms and structures of society, and this is the subject of the next chapter.

5

Coming back to ourselves

Alienation: lost in what we are not

Just before eleven o'clock at night the supermarket staff, with the industrial efficiency of a few swift movements, scrape all the buns off the shelves into black bin bags. Made just this morning, this food is now out of date, litter, something in the way. When I ask the staff why they are doing this they tell me there is a policy from head office to be followed. Here is a business that appears to have no pride in what it does, or love for the food it sells. Nor does it trust its staff to make their own decisions about their workplace; if they defied the policy they would be fired. In this place, food is just something to make money out of or throw away; so, it seems, are the staff. The worth of each is defined entirely by the use to which it may be put, and upon this the success of the business depends.

I would like to find an independent baker who loves to make bread and hates to throw it away, but here in affluent Uxbridge there is no such place. There are plenty of shops – over 300, mostly chains, of which 100 sell clothes – but outside the weekly market, no baker. Nor is there an independent grocer, butcher or fishmonger. There is no theatre, regular concert venue, central play area for kids, museum or art gallery. The town centre is arranged like a henge around two large shopping centres. A small stand of trees between them has been cut down; without the trees, the council says, it is easier for people to walk out of one centre and see the other opposite. In the intermediate space the town's only work of public sculpture, *Anticipation*, depicts a family apparently on their way to the shops.

Derby, Doncaster, Exeter, Sheffield, Swindon and most other towns have, like Uxbridge, been cosmetically 'regenerated' in the same fashion. If we asked ourselves, deeply, what values we wanted our community spaces to reflect, would we hand them over to big businesses? They know that there is money in 'fast fashion' clothes and not hand-baked bread, and that economic efficiency lies in making excess product and throwing it away rather than running out of it before the sale can be made. But the consequence of a town with 100 clothes shops and no independent baker or grocer is not just aesthetically depleted spaces – plastic places, ugly to be in – but ill health. Bread not loved in the making is not loved in the eating, and when we don't love what we eat our bodies suffer. In spending an average of £1,000 a year on new clothes, we take care of how we look, but in eating badly we show less interest in what we are. A quarter of the population (and nearly a third of children) are clinically obese.[114] The government response is a public education campaign on healthy diet, but the primary cause of obesity is not feckless personal choices but a system that privileges capital over people.

If we suffer as individuals by this system, we also suffer as communities. The term 'community' is generally used to mean a group of people resident in a locality, whether or not any communing goes on there. The Old English *gemœncipe*, meaning 'community', was defined by certain qualities of group relationship: fellowship, union and common ownership. In places like Uxbridge, the communing community is pushed into the spaces in which big business has no interest. Churches and town halls might still be on the High Street but only because they got there before we thought of shopping centres, and even capitalism finds them hard to shift.

The political-economic system largely defines the worth of a municipal space by its facility for generating profit for big business, rather than nurturing the overall well-being of a community. The shopping centres spring up, the independent bakers sell up or go bust and the supermarkets junk good food by the skipload because more money can be made that way. In this condition our communities are alienated from who and what we really are and promise to become. The things that genuinely matter most to us are pushed to the margins.

The theologian Carter Heyward argues that alienation is our basic human condition; we are thrown into it from birth.[115] For the educationalist Paulo Freire, whatever alienates disenfranchises us of our humanity, and so takes us away from our common vocation of becoming a humanised and humanising society. By cultivating awareness of alienation the genesis of violence is better understood. The main reason it gets a chapter in this book, however, is that nothing else so effectively stops us from recognising our shared peace-making vocation. Peace depends on us being what we are as humane human beings, and on putting what matters most to us at the centre of our lives and societies rather than neglecting it at the margins. In the kinds of alienation described here we are not only removed from the dignity of our being but also convinced that this broken relationship is a right one. As consumers, for example, rather than wondering why we cannot buy a good loaf of bread we crowd into the clothes shops and empty our pockets there. And the more alienated we are, the less available we are for making the choices that create the right relationships that are peace.

An assessment of modern society as entirely alienated would be a depressing and simplistic caricature; wherever people are able to relate well, alienation has no home. We play football in the park, talk about childbirth as a sort of miracle, and create music, arts and play out of almost nothing; the creativity and love of human beings are resilient. But forms of alienation are pervasive. In Britain, for example, the three most common causes of bodily harm are poor diet, insufficient exercise and smoking. Two thirds of us eat badly (indicated by a diet with insufficient fruit and vegetables), two thirds do not exercise enough and a fifth smoke.[116] Nor are our bodies made to sit in front of computers all day preparing spreadsheets and reports, or indeed writing books about peace. By these measures most of us are significantly alienated from our bodies.

Alienation is a feature of work, too. For a large minority, work is part of an industrial, largely semi-automated process; machinery operators and sales workers are the most likely of all occupational groups to find their work meaningless.[117] Others are forced by circumstance to fight to keep oppressive jobs; the poorest paid are the most likely to be chronically fearful of the sack.[118] As Marx would have predicted, self-employed workers are the most satisfied occupational group; employees with little autonomy in large, top-down businesses are the least satisfied.[119]

After work we spend most of our waking time watching television, the typical home's *axis mundi*. We spend an average of 3.8 hours per day in front of the box, or 19 years of our waking lives, making it more popular than spending time with friends.[120] TV can connect us with the world and offer true enjoyment and learning, but game shows overwhelmingly dominate the ratings.[121] Perhaps it is a way for a family to come together, then, but one survey found that only a fifth of parents regarded TV as 'quality time' with family, and about the same proportion said it was an obstacle.[122] Children watch around 10,000 violent acts on TV each year,[123] which normalises and trivialises violence, alienating young minds from what it really is.

Perhaps Western society's most characteristic form of alienation is consumerism: the rampant desire to acquire. It is a fetish: a lifeless thing invested with almost supernatural power to meet fundamental needs easily. Any existential itch can be scratched: if we lack self-esteem, friendship, a sense of belonging or even a sense of life's meaning, then a product exists to take the pain away. "We don't make cars," an advertisement (for cars!) proclaims, "we make joy."[124] Children will watch over 20,000 adverts like this a year, although they cannot normally know a marketing message for what it is until they are 11 or 12.[125] National Consumer Council research found that "the average ten year-old has internalised 300 to 400 brands – perhaps twenty times the number of birds in the wild that they could name".[126]

The psychoanalyst Adam Phillips argues that the main function of consumerism is to enable us to hide from ourselves.[127] Its alienating power is in offering subtle, addictive self-medication while perpetuating a sense of personal lack. Big businesses marshal huge financial resources to convince us of our deficiency, convince us that they can rectify it, and then convince us to part with our money. In this way, consumerism promises what the poet Wendell Berry calls an "ever-fugitive wholeness" while fragmenting both ourselves and the Earth.[128] As I write, even Greenpeace is encouraging us to start Christmas shopping early. Why would an organisation committed to tackling climate change do this? Because they have their own gift catalogue and a new biodegradable credit card that automatically transfers a small portion of every purchase to the charity so you can "defend our world while you shop".[129]

With consumerism goes materialism: excessive attachment to money and possessions. In 1970 less than half of new students at the University of California said becoming "very well off financially" was a very important motivation for their studies. By 1998 that proportion had risen to three quarters, outranking motivators such as "developing a meaningful philosophy of life", "helping others in need" and "becoming an authority in my field".[130] Research shows that when we privilege materialist pursuits over others our well-being suffers; one study found that materialist values indicated a greater likelihood of all ten psychological disorders tested, of which the strongest link was with dependency.[131] People who rank highly on a scale of materialist values are also more likely to be possessive, non-generous, envious, stressed, non-empathic, poorer at relating to others, insecure, over-consuming and less autonomous in their choices.[132]

The British political system is also an alienated one, as it must be when 18 of the 23-member Cabinet are millionaires, whose opulent privilege cannot but estrange them from the people they ostensibly represent.[133] Chancellor George Osborne's claim that the costs of deep cuts in public services will be borne mostly by "those with the broadest shoulders" is absurd from the point of view of a minimum-wage cleaner emptying the office bins at Canary Wharf.[134] Tony Blair once said that only through solidarity, social justice and "a strong society of others" can individuals find fulfilment and bond us in our common humanity; he now owns nine homes.[135] The MP expenses scandal of 2009 was epitomised by Peter Viggers' disallowed claim for the £1,600 cost of a duck island for his mansion's pond.[136] This should not surprise; when a millionaire MP buys a stately home in the country and then a French chateau for holidays, he has already put himself before the people he represents.

This is not to suggest that the ruling elite are bad people, indifferent to the injustices of the world; apart from their excess of privilege they are not much different from the rest of us. The issue is that justice is something they are interested in rather than simply in, otherwise they would not have the property portfolios they do. At the same time, these are the people we vote for; more than one of my acquaintances voted for Boris Johnson for the London mayoralty for no other reason than that he was funny on *Have I Got News for You*. This whimsical approach to the vote is not democracy but the subtle tyranny of a politically alienated society.

The territory that alienation occupies proceeds from our hearts and minds and rolls out to encompass our bodies, living rooms, workplaces, localities, societies and the Earth. Whilst a problem in its own right, alienation also keeps us from taking the ubiquity of violence seriously. Poverty, war, climate change, a lost sense of the sacred, and religious fanaticism all have alienation in common. How will a child who knows 20 times as many brands as birds take climate change seriously? How will a student who rates being well off over living meaningfully or helping others in need use their skills and knowledge in a socially useful way? How will someone who really believes that car manufacturers sell joy recognise the true sources of joy in the world? How will a wealthy individualist be in solidarity with people born into poverty and violence? How can someone who votes for the most handsome candidate in a General Election TV debate be politically responsible? As Iain Crichton Smith wrote, alienation turns each of us into an "unreal person in an unreal place".[137] There is no cognitive reason why we should not know each bird's song as well as we know our Starbucks from our McDonalds. Until we do, I think Crichton Smith's value judgement will stand.

Our alienations are a form of forgetfulness of who and what we are as individuals and communities. In this fashion they prepare the way for violence, which we cannot respond to fully once our humanity has been diminished. Alienation and violence are two sides of the same coin – or credit card – and where alienation goes, violence is not far behind. For in order to perpetrate violence against a neighbour – to strip them of their true name and label them 'enemy' – we need first to be alienated from their dignity as a human being.

In high-tech warfare, so-called stand-off weaponry such as cruise missiles ($1m a piece) and drones ($9m) can be deployed anywhere in the world and controlled from Nevada, thousands of miles of alienation away. Similarly, people who run the arms trade will never meet the people their work affects; they will drive home, tend the lawn and tuck their kids into bed. Long ago they will have left their "conscience at the door", as one former BAE Systems executive put it, for a lucrative career facilitating violence.[138] BAE presents its careers to new graduates as opportunities to learn from the natural world and create machines that fly as effortlessly as birds. "[P]erfect performance in nature is a great source of inspiration for our people," says the careers ad, "It's a question of instinct."[139] The Ministry of Defence has commissioned a toy-maker to design 'realistic' soldier figures for British toddlers. The government claims bizarrely that playing with the toys "promotes things like discipline, sense of belonging to a wider organisation and team work"[140] but they are really a way to alienate children from the realities of war with a view to recruiting them later on. In each case – high-tech warfare, the arms trade, military recruitment – alienation marches ahead of the violence.

Preparing for peace: confronting spiritual violence

In an alienated condition we are by definition estranged from a right relationship with the world, ourselves, and the very question of what matters most. The examples of alienation described here violate our common being, and like violence have their roots in political and economic structures, psychology, social values and cultural norms.

There is a further characteristic of alienation that is of particular importance from a perspective of faith: its roots in our self-enthronement at the centre of our universe. Consider food again. If I enthrone myself at the centre of the universe, I make myself sovereign over all, while my rival neighbour does the same. From my 'throne', the world's resources are laid out below for me to seize, possess and dispose of as I wish. As the presumptive sovereign, this is my *entitlement*. If I have sufficient power I can acquire tons of food and waste it with impunity because it is mine, not yours, however hungry you may be.

If I begin to enter a kind of faithfulness that recognises life as *given*, then I begin to see that food is part of that givenness. I see that my own life, even as I sit on the throne of my universe, is also given. This means that in this universe of mine something comes before me, which I do not rule over and to which I properly belong. Whatever throne I think I am sitting on, I now realise it is not at the centre of the universe.

As this *metanoia* process unfolds, it effects a sort of universal *coup d'état* in which I willingly cede my throne to what gives life. It is a shaky revolution because I can and do take the throne back, repeatedly. Even so, from my new vantage point I might see that food, as part of the same givenness of life, is something for me to be thankful for, rather than an object of my sovereignty. If the givenness of life comes before my own ego desires, then food is given for me to use (and in this sense it is mine) but not possess, and in this sense it is not mine. Crucially, this means that if I have more food than I can use, the surplus is not mine to possess and should be returned, which in practice means offering it where it is needed. I am not entitled to the surplus, and so returning the food to where it is needed is not charity, because it is not mine to give away, but justice.

So, when I witness the supermarket staff throwing away good food I want to respond not only because an injustice is being committed to the hungry, or because of the ecological damage of waste, important though those are, but because I see food as a sacred, given thing. The surplus food is not the supermarket's to throw away, and so the practice is, to my mind, theft. As theft, it violates the givenness of our common being: "It is not mine, it is not theirs, it is God's."

The violation of the sacred – that is, desecration – is what we might call spiritual violence. Whilst harming no-one and no thing directly, it manifests physically through violence in the world. In the UK we throw away millions of tonnes of food in a year with the impunity that depends entirely on a presumption of entitlement to do so. The same presumption allows City of London traders to gamble huge quantities of food on the futures market, pushing global prices beyond reach of the world's poorest people.

From the point of view that takes life and thus food to be given, the supermarket throwaway and global food speculation are part of the same sacrilegious doing, in which something sacred is defiled and destroyed by an an act of violence leading to further violence. Food is but one example. Slavery is made possible by a similar process of desecration that presumes human life to be tradable rather than sacred, an end in itself. Indeed, the same presumption facilitates all kinds of violation, for violence always turns the being of our neighbour, or the Earth, or ourselves, into something less than sacred – less, that is, than it really is.

We do not need to be religious in the usual sense of the word to have a feeling for the sacredness of life. Yet in a largely secular society a feeling for what is sacred is, by definition, not a commonly shared experience, let alone one guiding how we live and organise our societies. Does recognising a blackbird's song matter more than knowing what 'skinny decaf latte' means? In a world where a feeling for what is sacred is not generally considered important, this question is a matter of personal preference alone. In other words, without a feeling for the sacredness of the natural world, why should I give a damn about the birds? Unless we recognise life as a given and therefore sacred thing, I think we are bound to fall into violence.

In this light, Rowan Williams' observation in a lecture on climate change makes a great deal of sense:

> ...so much of what's wrong has its roots in a shared cultural and spiritual crisis. The nature of that crisis could be summed up rather dramatically by saying it's a loss of a sense of what life is... We are disconnected and we need to be reintroduced to life.[141]

As Rowan Williams suggests, preventing the violence of runaway climate change will depend not only on harnessing renewable energy and consuming less, but also on being grounded in a shared feeling for what life is really about. A challenge of ecologically informed peacemaking is therefore to create conditions where driving to the shops or flying to France for a quick holiday is not felt to belong to a life and society committed to the dignity of our common being.

By holding faith with life as a sacred thing, we can hope to hold all our choices, even the pragmatic ones, within the same life-giving, life-affirming commitment. In this way, faith communities, being concerned with our humaneness and vibrancy and with a feeling for what is sacred, can inspire a journey out of alienation into deeper freedom. The threshold of this change is always right in front of us, as this poem by Kaye Lee suggests:

Beyond

Through the locked door is life,
at least, this is the rumour passed
in whispers, under cover of dark:
who dares to lift the key that hangs
like a decapitated moonbeam nailed
to the door frame, and turns it
in the lock to release the black bolt

so the door swings open, will lead
all of us into bright-eyed day.

Each night we watch each other,
lying on our lumpy pillows. Who
will be the first to try? Who wants
to leave this grey safety so badly
they'll brave the threat of a truth
not of our dreaming? Each night,
one by one, we fall into sleep, still
facing the door we never open.[142]

When a person, community or nation braves "the threat of a truth not of our dreaming" and starts to peel back the layers of alienation, they create pockets of freedom, upsetting the alienating systems and norms of society and making peace more possible.

Preparing for peace: making space to be ourselves

In 1920s and 1930s New York, an African American family struggling to pay the bills would organise a party for their neighbourhood. Everyone from the street would drop a small entrance fee into a pot to help with the rent. They would crowd into the apartment, enjoy a big meal and dance for the rest of the night. In the morning the world outside still regarded African Americans as subhuman – nothing on that level had changed – but for one night the community created its own freedom.

Their dance developed into the Lindy Hop, an exuberant, earthy partnered dance that Europeans like me are learning today to the same Harlem jazz. London's smart-shirted office workers pitch up at the dance class, at first stiff-limbed and clumsy. Those who get that this is a dance about freedom rather than getting the steps right become more fluid and creative, progressively released from the invisible straitjacket into which sitting in front of a screen all day has locked their bodies. Once the social dancing kicks in after the class the room becomes a pulsing mass of bodies improvising to the music. In a small way the dance returns us to what matters most: those joys and passions that are real.

In David LaChapelle's extraordinary documentary film *Rize* some young people in South Central Los Angeles have turned to dance as a way of belonging and being free within the oppressive injustices of their social environment. The district has the highest homicide rate in the city: four people are murdered every week, almost all by gunshot. Latino and black people in their late teens and early twenties are the main victims.[143] The dance groups, combined with the resilience of their church-centred community, have helped young people find a way to survive gangland without being in a gang: for many of the dancers in *Rize*, the choice had come down to joining one or the other. The Krumps are one of the dance groups. They have turned the violence from their own lives into a cathartic dance, during which they throw each other against a fence or wall or squirm on the floor as if they are being beaten; they get bruised but the apparent violence is a form of unusual play and no-one gets really hurt. Another group do their street dancing in clowning make-up; each dancer crafts their own mask to suit their personality, playfully subverting the surrounding violence.

Like the Harlem rent parties, these dance communities do not transform the injustices of the world but they do create a space where the alienation of their environment, for a time, has been largely overcome. One of the Clowns, Tight Eyez, explains how dancing helped save his community from becoming empty vessels for commercial culture to fill:

> We're not gonna be clones of the commercial hip-hop world... because that's been seen for so many years...
> [A]nother generation of kids with morals and values

... won't need ... what's being commercialized or tailor-
made for them... And we're of more value than any
piece of jewellery... or any car or any big house that
anybody could buy.[144]

Perhaps a key phrase here is "won't need", which is meant, I
think, prophetically. Tight Eyez is saying that his dance community
gives his generation a space to be themselves, realise what matters
most to them, and recognise their own value as human beings.
Commercialised, alienating culture stops being interesting
because in these conditions it is unneeded. The most powerful,
most concise criticism of consumer culture I know is not that it
is morally wrong or ecologically disastrous, but was the message
of a sticker plastered over some inane, unremembered advert on
London's Underground: "Capitalism is boring". Once we know
what matters most and what we truly need, Oxford Street becomes
the most boring mile on Earth.

Tight Eyez is saying something else prophetic, too – "we're of
more value" than anything we can possess. Like all prophetic
utterances this shifts the axis of the universe back to where it
should be: away from the alienated, commercialised world that
has been fed to the youth of America and towards the sufficiency
of their own dignity as human beings.

Paulo Freire wrote that personal and social change begins when
"the oppressed" become critically aware of their oppression and
how they have internalised and passively accepted it. Only by
this shift in awareness, which he called conscientisation, can they
begin to recover their "stolen humanity" and become participants
in re-making the world – subjects of history rather than only its
objects.[145] Freire's insight was that, like Tight Eyez, we need to
become sufficiently free from oppression in our consciousness
before we can overcome it in the world; we need to know how we
are alienated before beginning to break free of it.

The Harlem rent parties, the Los Angeles Clowns and Krumps and London's Lindy Hoppers all create pockets of bodily and spiritual freedom where the axis of the universe is moved slightly closer to the things that matter most. At their best, Quakers and other faith communities are trying to do the same; we all have our own ways of dancing. In an extensively alienated world we need our faith traditions to number among the pockets of disalienated, genuinely faithful humanity. By supporting us to be a little more aware, vibrant, humane and free, faith communities can help prepare us for a vocation of serving the dignity of our common being. The next chapter explores what this work might mean in practice, based on love of one's self and one's community, love of one's neighbour or one's neighbour's community, and love of the sacred givenness of life.

6

Creating peace

For Quakers and others of a peace-making faith, hope is focused here and now, in the world, rather than in some far-away, heavenly realm of the future. What kind of practice might this involve us in? Karen Armstrong tells a story about Rabbi Hillel, a Pharisaic sage in the first century:

> It was said that one day a pagan had approached Hillel and promised to convert to Judaism if he could summarise the entire Torah while he stood on one leg. Standing on one leg, Hillel replied: "What is hateful to yourself, do not do to your fellow man. That is the whole of the Torah and the remainder is but commentary. Go study it."[146]

Apparently quite separately from Hillel's tradition Jesus was teaching the same:

> "Love the Lord your God with all your heart and with all your soul and with all your mind." This is the first and greatest commandment. And the second is like it:

"Love your neighbour as yourself." All the Law and the
Prophets hang on these two commandments.[147]

Augustine followed: the discipleship of every Christian is to
love God, he wrote, and to love our neighbours as ourselves rather
than to squabble over doctrine, for everything that Moses had
written was for this love.[148] If the concern of a peace-making faith
is to ask what makes relationships 'right' then here we are told
that a threefold love – of God, self and neighbour – is the way.

For the theologian Carter Heyward, what counts in love is not
so much a feeling of affection as a practical commitment to the
relationship.[149] Love is something made real by doing; indeed, it is
something to do on days when we do not feel it with neighbours
we might not necessarily like. This is to approach relationships
with the authenticity that holding faith with life can lead into,
where being true to a relationship and bringing love to it are the
same thing.

Love of God

What, then, might be a practical commitment to a right relationship with God? One answer is that love of God begins with
honouring the dignity and vibrancy of the life that is given – to
make good with the gift. The loving mother or father is a peace-
maker in this sense, so is the joiner who loves wood, the midwife
who still feels the magic of delivering babies, the cook who insists
on seasonal vegetables, the farmer who still loves the land, the
friends who enjoy listening to each other, the strangers who greet
each other in curiosity, and the activists who stand up for life in
the face of its violation. However fragmented the world might
otherwise seem, all these participate "in that time of creation",
to borrow Rebecca Solnit's words, restoring a right relationship
with the life that is given.[150]

For a fuller honouring of life, three disciplines of faith may be useful. One is wonder. Speaking personally, I commit to peace not first because violence is shocking, although that gives sufficient reason, but because I am moved by the simple wonder of being alive on a planet with breathable air and 30 million species of life. The profusion and integrity of life makes violence shocking. It might seem odd to think of wonder as a discipline but how often do we look up from what we are doing to give it space? If I lose sight of this, and I often do, then I lose something of what life is really about; something which my commitment to peace needs in order to persist in a violent world. Without this wonder – this existential 'yes' – a commitment to peace can become moralistic, sombre and as alienating as the alienation it seeks to overcome.

A second discipline is thanksgiving. According to P. V. Rajagopal, it is usual for Indian land activists to begin their meetings with a prayer giving thanks in turn to the water, the land, and the forest that lie at the heart of their livelihoods.[151] The activists' thanksgiving recognises that these three life-giving elements, on which they and we are entirely dependent, are given. To give thanks in this way is to bow to the necessity of grace – to honour that which, as sacred and life-giving, rightly comes before our own egos in the universe. In other words it is to honour the miraculous, if we hold with its ancient meaning: an event leading us to smile or be astonished with wonder. Even offering thanks for the essentially miraculous nature of waking up in the morning is a way of loving life as grace.

An earlier chapter suggested in passing that many people of faith experience grace as an energy working around and through them. My own feeling, and I think it is widely shared among other people of a peace-making faith, is that the power that gives life is already at work creating peace in the world. When a ten year-old child is amazed at a blackbird, it is not by the power of her own will or at least not solely that, but by the grace of life already abundant in the universe. It is this grace that enables the same child to ask, as one did when I was running a session about local ecology at a Leeds school, "Why are the grown-ups killing the world?" A peace-making faith can do no more than participate in this ever present creativity. Many artists feel the same, as do many loving parents who hold a new-born baby for the first time: their creative work is far from only their own. This, then, is a third discipline in the love of God.

An essential purpose of worship is to gather the faith community around this threefold discipline: to wonder at the givenness of life, offer thanks and, crucially, allow it to enter more fully into our own lives and world. In this way, worship is the root that nourishes a peace-making faith. And as for the Indian land activists, so for Quakers, worship is not confined to a building; potentially every corner of life is religious space and every moment sacramental. It is there in the water, land and forest on which our lives depend. It is there, too, in each other; the Quaker peace-worker Adam Curle wrote that we should "praise in our friends the manifestation of divine qualities" as an "act of worship" and "act of service".[152]

A faith commitment to peace assumes the wholeness and fullness of this shared and given life, in which every person, community, people and ecosystem has inalienable value as part of the whole. This hope for the world begins to manifest in the peace-making community as it gradually assumes a new 'shape', known to people with Christian roots as gospel order. The hope is that the growing faithfulness of the community will reflect in the way it acts and is organised, which will then show up in the world as a testimony to its faith. In this way, a peace-making community will come to embody (or incarnate) its vision for a *shalom* world. Gospel order is a road to travel; what matters is not where we are on the road but whether we are on it at all. Many faith groups including Quaker ones are beset with their own petty politics and buried conflicts, but if the hope of gospel order is shared, and passionately so, then these are simply the challenges we would expect on the way.

Recalling Jesus' words, to love God is "the first and greatest commandment".[153] It comes before, albeit as part of, making peace in the world. Why should this be so when our neighbour's needs for love seem greater than any god's? The reason, I think, has to do with the revolutionary perspective of faith, in which 'God', and not our own egos, is at the centre of the universe. From this vantage point, the world looks different and requires a distinctive response. In an essay on economics, the poet Wendell Berry points out that when we have regard to God first, we see that the Earth is its own economy, which precedes and contains our everyday economy. We need to start with the divine economy based on the Earth's life-giving integrity in order to relate authentically and critically to what we normally think of as 'the economy', in which the integrity of the Earth is not a consideration. Wendell Berry's prophetic perspective is made possible by his humane faith, in which regard is first paid to love of, or a right relationship to, God.

A love of God is reflected in the common Quaker affirmations, "there is that of God in every person" and "the whole of life is sacramental". Both flow from a feeling for the promise of life, its abundant grace and its possibility of peace, and both can bring us time and again back to thankfulness. Yet they are not for saying lightly. Almost everywhere life is compromised. Some young people wake up every day to parents who are addicted to drugs, will steal their pocket money for their next fix and will have taken the belt to them or worse by the time evening comes. This situation, more common than most of us realise, hardly seems sacramental, and its degradation is nothing to thank God for. Unless this challenges us, the affirmation of "that of God in every person" is no more than a platitude. It requires courage and imagination not to shrink from such violence and to look for where, beneath the wreckage and rubble of the most oppressed situations, the promise of life might be found persisting. Such is the responsibility that attends the affirmation of "that of God in every person".

This is an uncertain search, full of the doubt of a living faith, but full also of its trust and hope. In an Alternatives to Violence Project workshop Kevin tells us he gets into rages with his wife. He has not hit her, he says, but on several occasions he has smashed up something in the room or put his fist through a door. He knows he is out of control when he does this and says he hates himself for it. He doesn't know how to stop himself; when his anger reaches a certain pitch he just flips. His wife is too frightened to live with him and has thrown him out of the house so he is now living alone. When they married they did love each other, and he thinks that maybe somewhere tangled up in this mess she still loves him and he still loves her, although he can't be sure. This is his side of the story. We don't know the name of his wife and we don't know what his story leaves out, yet as he speaks, this big working man is visibly struggling not to break down. He has nowhere to go and no-one he can trust to talk to. Sometimes of an evening, he says, he drives out from the city to the Cotswold Hills and parks at a favourite spot. He looks out across the vast vale below and feels a little peace. It's such a beautiful spot, he says; it helps to be in such a beautiful place.

If we are committed to turning our lives towards peace then, like Kevin, we need to find and feel the grace of such life-giving places, people and happenings. This feeling for what life can be – its promise – can charge the universe with possibility and inspire real, practical hope. Even so, we will keep resisting having our lives turned around. It is a process that, as Joanna Macy has suggested, proceeds in stages: from indifference to fear, denial, grief, despair, anger, guilt, hope, action and, finally, change.[154] That needs patience and determination in equal measure, as well as courage and honesty. Yet the shaken are shaken because they resisted this process of *metanoia*, were overcome by it, then started to live within it. We might choose to understand this – metaphorically or literally – as a constant tussle with a God wiser and stronger than we are. For those of us who feel a sense of life's givenness, this 'God' is found in such flesh-and-blood sacramental moments of everyday life as Kevin's. The more we notice them and give thanks, the closer we might move to the heart and source of peace, as *shalom*.

Love of self

The essence of much Christian teaching on personal life is to become small enough for God. We are supposed to make a virtue of modesty, exercising restraint in our positive self-regard rather than celebrating ourselves as part of God's work. At its worst a Christian insistence on modesty brands believers, like the clothes advert brands shoppers, as not good enough, which is a subtle form of violence.

The Anglican Prayer of Humble Access includes the words: "We are not worthy even to gather up the crumbs under your table, but it is your nature always to have mercy."[155] The inspiration for the passage is the Gospel of Mark, chapter 7, where the table symbolises salvation.[156] The intention is to show that our deliverance depends on the grace of mercy, for we are sinners and need help beyond our own prideful assumptions of self-sufficiency. In this sense it is a powerful utterance, capable of leaving us 'shaken' and bringing us closer to a right relationship to God and the Earth. But how often is it understood as such? How often, rather, does it reinforce our doubts that we are not good enough for God or the world and confirm us in a sense of worthlessness?

If our faith leaves us hating ourselves then it generates the very conditions of violence that it seeks to overcome. The error is a confusion of sinfulness with worthlessness. Yet they are not the same; indeed they are opposites. If I am worthless, why should I care how sinful I am? Rather, it is because our lives have worth that we should take our sinfulness seriously. Humility before our sin has nothing to do with self-effacing modesty or (worse) self-hating guilt; no-one is served well by lives etiolated by lack of self-love. Rather, being humble means recognising the radical equality of all being; as Carter Heyward describes it, it is "…to know ourselves as no more or less valuable than anyone else in the world".[157] After all, the commandment is to love our neighbour as ourselves, not *instead of* ourselves. "I am come that they might have life, and that they might have it more abundantly," Jesus said.[158]

Love of self does not gloss over our sins, nor can it substitute for our need for grace and the *metanoia* of repentance. But it does allow for what the counsellor Brian Thorne calls "appropriate guilt".[159] Unlike its self-hating form, guilt that is "appropriate" recognises and accepts mistakes and cherishes our lives as worth the course corrections they need to become more authentic. In other words, appropriate guilt is a form of appropriate pride – not the swaggering hubris of 'better than you' but the affirmation of what we are and can become.

Learning how to love our neighbour and ourselves go together; why be generous in one and parsimonious in the other, why leave one's self out of one's own passion for peace? Yet whilst love of neighbour is considered a virtue, self-love is often confused with selfishness or self-centredness when it need be nothing of the sort. The selfish self or community puts itself at the centre of the universe and indulges in facile satisfactions that substitute for real love. Like a spoilt child, the selfish self wants for nothing except the most necessary thing of all: to love and be loved. An out-and-out selfish person's tragic condition is not that he loves himself too much but that he has not yet learnt to love himself at all.

In the peace of *shalom* each of us belongs on Earth and in society; each of us belongs to the dignity of being that is peace. To love oneself is perhaps first to accept this, which means to treat one's self – warts, wonders and all – as an object worthy of one's own loving, and of others' loving, and of God's loving. The non-selfish, self-loving person or community does not confuse the false want to be liked with the genuine need to be met as an equal with others. Self-love cherishes genuine longings and stands up for them, keeping faith with one's own peace in the face of the alienation and violence of the world. It was often said of Gandhi that although he was often outwardly humiliated, much of his power in nonviolence came from steadfastly retaining his dignity in the face of oppression: we may endure humiliation, he said, but we should not cooperate with it.[160] Similarly, during the civil rights struggle, to every social prejudice that told them they were less than human, African Americans often responded with "God made me and said it was good". Let us all wake up every morning with this on our lips and thankfulness in our selves.

That said, self-love is not easy. In a society that tells us in one breath that we are not good enough and in another that at least we are better than them over there, learning to love ourselves is something to dare to do. It is a matter of keeping who we truly are "alive and present", says the Buddhist monk Thich Nhat Hanh:

> All of us, children and adults, are beautiful flowers. Our eyelids are exactly like rose petals, especially when our eyes are closed. Our ears are like morning glories listening to the sounds of the birds. Our lips form a beautiful flower every time we smile. And our two hands are a lotus flower with five petals. The practice is to keep our "flowerness" alive and present, not just for our own benefit but for the happiness of everyone.[161]

The poetry of self-love is particularly eloquent in the work of Walt Whitman. His direct, casual regard for himself and others is as fresh as a spring morning. Here are a few lines from *Song of Myself*, in which he affirms himself and all as part of the "perfect fitness and equanimity of things" – no more, no less:

> Sure as the most certain sure . . . . plumb in the
> uprights, well entretied, braced in the beams,
> Stout as a horse, affectionate, haughty, electrical,
> I and this mystery here we stand.
>
> Clear and sweet is my soul . . . . and clear and sweet is
> all that is not my soul.
>
> Lack one lacks both . . . . and the unseen is proved by
> the seen,
> Till that becomes unseen and receives proof in its
> turn.
>
> Showing the best and dividing it from the worst, age
> vexes age,
> Knowing the perfect fitness and equanimity of things,
> while they discuss I am silent, and go bathe and
> admire myself.
>
> Welcome is every organ and attribute of me, and of
> any man hearty and clean,
> Not an inch nor a particle of an inch is vile, and none
> shall be less familiar than the rest.[162]

A love of self, as part of a commitment to peace, bends towards an abundant daily life in all its aspects. Consider our relationship to food again; we spend about ten years of our waking lives preparing and eating it. How might love of self be expressed through food? Not in checking whether the organic, bio-degradably packaged, microwave-ready meal and its list of nutritional contents ticks the ethical box. A love of self implies a love of good food, and whatever the packet says there is nothing good about sterile, salty, ready-meal mush, and our bodies know it.

Really caring about food – about what it is, where it comes from, what our relationship with it is, and how to enjoy it – involves us in its processes, of which the eating is but one part. In practice, this might mean growing the ingredients ourselves or knowing the grower personally; preparing the food with care and enjoyment; and eating the food with thanks and pleasure. By caring about the ingredients, local and seasonal food is preferred over anything air-freighted, and the farmers' market or independent shop is preferred over the supermarket. By caring how the food is eaten, it is enjoyed at a table with others rather than in front of the TV. In a small way, eating well brings us into the fullness of life, less alienated from our bodies, from our family, from our local community and from the rhythms and processes of the Earth. Big business and intensive agriculture are less likely to get our money, too, so there is a political dimension to this commitment to food. When time and care are taken over how we meet our need for food, the result is a better meal, better enjoyed.

Are other areas of our lives also self-loving? Love of self might mean choosing to travel by bike or train or bus, not mainly because these are more ecologically sustainable, although that is sufficient reason, but because routine plane or car travel can take away the pleasure and adventure of the journey. And if the ageing process is welcomed as part of the sacred trajectory of life rather than constantly staved off, we might not shore up our mortal selves with ephemera or, in the case of some political leaders, try to make an immortal mark on history by going to war. At issue, then, is not first whether our lives meet a certain ethical standard but whether we live in life-giving ways, involved in life-giving processes that overcome alienation and restore us to a right relationship to ourselves and others. If this comes first, the ethics will follow.

This love of – that is, commitment to – the rhythms and processes of daily life is often criticised as middle-class privilege; a world of allotments and bicycles that misunderstands the needs of people in poverty. It can but does not have to be this. It is a conceit to assume that people in material poverty are not, or could not be, interested in eating well; this is surely important for everyone on Earth. Nor need a concern for the Earth's processes be a naïve, back-to-nature policy. There is nothing about eating well or travelling slowly that harks back to a mythical golden age; it is simply a way to live more vibrantly right in the middle of the alienated conditions of modern life.

All that said – and it is easily said from a position of relative privilege – economic structures powerfully condition our behaviours. By manufacturing needs and wants, a corporate-capitalist economic system displaces a shared sense of what matters most so that big business can commandeer our time and money. When a pair of trainers is made by a child for pennies in Shanghai and sold for £100 as a status symbol for a bullied teenager in Manchester, the relationship of big business to the poorest people is one of parasitism. Certainly, economic structures need to change in order to wrest a larger social space for life-affirming, life-giving ways of being, yet that should not let us off the hook of trying to make better choices now. At the Giant Veggie Patch in Manchester, for example, a community is growing its own food together: people are getting to know neighbours, bypassing the supermarkets, saving money and enjoying good food. The guiding question is simply this: how can we reconnect with what matters most in our lives and the processes that make this possible? The answers will be varied and sometimes contradictory but we can still begin with the question, whoever we are and whatever our circumstances.

Love of neighbour

Re-imagining our neighbour

The Parable of the Good Samaritan is Jesus' response to an expert in Jewish law who wants to test him. "Teacher," asks the expert, "what must I do to inherit eternal life?" Jesus asks the man to recite the law and he does so: "'Love the Lord your God with all your heart and with all your soul and with all your strength and with all your mind"; and, "Love your neighbour as yourself."' But the man wants to push Jesus and so he asks, "And who is my neighbour?" The story continues:

> In reply Jesus said: "A man was going down from Jerusalem to Jericho, when he was attacked by robbers. They stripped him of his clothes, beat him and went away, leaving him half dead. A priest happened to be going down the same road, and when he saw the man, he passed by on the other side. So too, a Levite, when he came to the place and saw him, passed by on the other side. But a Samaritan, as he travelled, came where the man was; and when he saw him, he took pity on him. He went to him and bandaged his wounds, pouring on oil and wine. Then he put the man on his own donkey, brought him to an inn and took care of him. The next day he took out two denarii and gave them to the innkeeper. 'Look after him,' he said, 'and when I return, I will reimburse you for any extra expense you may have.'"

In the parable, Levites and priests represent authorities in Jewish practice and law, just like the man who is testing Jesus. They pass by the man but the Samaritan – considered a sworn enemy by the prevailing Jewish orthodoxy – tends him with assiduous care. When Jesus asks which of the three fulfilled the law, he puts his challenger firmly on the hook. The expert can see that the parable is really about him, for two authorities just like him – the Levite and the priest – ignored the injured man. The Samaritan, a complete outsider despised for his ignorance of God's law, does what should be done. The Samaritan is righteous not because he *thinks* the right thing about God as the expert does, but because he has *done* the right thing by God. Jesus' challenger has no choice but to admit that his enemy, the merciful Samaritan, is the true neighbour. Jesus tells him, "Go and do likewise."[163]

The Greek word used for neighbour in the New Testament is *plesion*, 'near', but Jesus uses the parable to show that those furthest away are also our neighbours. The parable is more than an exhortation to serve the needy. It tells us the supposed authorities on the law – that is, on how we should live – do not necessarily know it. It takes someone guided by a humane passion rather than expert knowledge to show what the law really means in practice. The Samaritan's heart shows us that love of neighbour means love of both Jew and gentile, for the Kingdom of God is open to everyone.

The parable widens our common understanding of a neighbour to include all people, but we now need to widen it in other ways, too. With our growing ecological awareness it is no longer sufficient, indeed it is hubristic, to recognise only human beings as our neighbours. That we belong to the Earth – and not the other way round – is what the Noah's Ark story has always been trying to tell us, says Rowan Williams: "Nothing could be clearer in the biblical text than the belief that humanity is meaningless seen independently of the world of diverse life-forms in which it is embedded."[164] He reminds us that God's covenant after the flood was not with human beings alone but with "every living creature on earth".[165]

If the neighbourhood includes all life then it must also include us, for we are no more and no less than a neighbour in society, on the Earth, in being. We belong as fellow participants in this vast body of being, neither above it nor below it but simply of it. The theologian Mary Grey terms this self-in-relation the "ecological self".[166] This means a self (or community) whose essence or identity is inseparable from its relationships with all around it, unlike the hubristic self that imagines itself independent and tries to gate itself off from its relationality. We are all involved (lit. 'rolled in') with one another's being.

Meeting our neighbour

The parable of the Samaritan is about creating a right relationship with our neighbour, not simply helping out. Nor is the Samaritan being merely charitable; if he were, he could have tossed some coins to the injured man and carried on home, never having looked him in the face but nonetheless enjoying a comfortable feeling of having done the right thing by God. This would have entrenched the power of the giver over the given-to and reinforced the social distance between the two. For the same reason, the Samaritan does not stand for the modern-day, self-justifying philanthropy of billionaires who turn the fruits of their aggressive, monopolistic capitalism into a palliative for the oppressed. This sort of paternalistic charity can preserve life, certainly, but it is only made possible by the life-destroying hoarding of wealth. Lower down the economic scale, and in form the same, is the increasingly popular practice of sending goats to Africa for Christmas. Perhaps more goats are needed in parts of Africa but if we think this gets us off the hook then we should think again, says Nigerian activist Justice Egware: "Poverty is about people… we're not asking for sympathy; we're asking for justice."[167]

In contrast, the Samaritan is standing with his neighbour's problem, struggle and hope. As with all true solidarity, the

Samaritan's response to the injured man says first that this problem is his own as well as his neighbour's, and second that they will face it together as the equals they really are, as his three ministrations testify. In pouring oil and wine on the man's wounds, he shows a physical tenderness for his neighbour that only a fellowship of equals makes possible. The message here is that love is only real when generous – poured out – and there is never such a thing as wasted love. He then recognises the man as his social equal by setting him on his own mount while walking alongside like a servant. In swapping their places the Samaritan has reversed the unequal social positions of the two men, showing that his neighbour is not the objectified 'helpless and needy' but his equal. And when the Samaritan leaves money with an inn-keeper to look after the man, he promises to "reimburse you for any extra expense you may have". Although he has left the injured man and is now distant (not the nearby neighbour of *plesion*), the Samaritan's commitment remains constant; the physical distance between people has no bearing on who counts as a neighbour.

In these three acts the Samaritan meets his neighbour as an equal, worthy of love; that is, as sharing the right to a right relationship. His gestures are political, too, for they re-order the structured social relationship between the two men and testify against the hypocrisy of convention and authority. On this reading, the parable stands for how we could meet all our neighbours who have less power than we do, bearing in mind that, writ large, our neighbourhood is the ecological society of the Earth.

The injured man is so disempowered by circumstance that he cannot even stand up; he receives the Samaritan's help silently and, we assume, passively. Of course, neighbours with power use it to meet their needs, often in ways that are in direct or indirect conflict with us and what matters to us. As the injured man in Jesus' parable well knows, those with power but without a commitment to their neighbour will sooner or later try to meet their needs violently. How might we meet a potentially violent neighbour while holding faith with a commitment to peace?

Facing potential violence is always a risk, whether the conflict is between next-door neighbours or nation states, but we are not devoid of the resources needed to respond well and without violence. Jesus' counsel, "Love your enemies"[168] is often taken to mean something like 'let those who antagonise you trample you down'. But if love means action that makes a right relationship, "Love your enemies" means putting your individual self or community in right relationship with those who oppose you. This is an attitude of assertiveness: standing up for your self and the self that opposes you, holding the dignity of both in creative tension with one another. "Love your enemies" is then an invitation to respond to conflict creatively and with authenticity.

Nothing makes love work harder than a conflict squarely faced in this way. When love is at work relationships can deepen, trust can grow and peace can be created. There are a thousand techniques for this but the heat of the moment seems to boil them down to one thing: an experiment in active respect for self and neighbour. Even the most apparently trivial conflicts are experienced as threatening and trigger fight-or-flight reactions, and so responding with respect is always courageous. It takes us slightly beyond ourselves into a space of hope and grace, which is perhaps exactly the place where people committed to the trust of faith need to be.

The Bible is concerned with the transformative potential of this same loving authenticity when faced with situations that are so severely challenging that hope seems unrealistic. How can we love both our own self and an oppressive neighbour when their outward power – personal, physical, social, political, economic – is far greater than ours? As is common in the Bible, the text tells us we have to go much further for peace than we think is reasonable and then, just as we are complaining of the impossibility of it all, promises the resources to do it.

Jesus uses metaphor to advise how to respond: go the second mile, give up your cloak and turn the other cheek. This might not seem like the most practical of advice but the text is once again showing us how to stand up for ourselves, create dilemmas for oppressors and publicly expose their unjust practices. According to the theologian Walter Wink, the law at the time allowed a Roman soldier to order a civilian to carry their pack for one mile but no further. By going the second mile, the civilian would force the soldier to break the law. Give your cloak to the man who takes your coat and you embarrass him with your nakedness in front of all, and implicate him in it. A back-handed slap to the face was a typical insult from the strong to the weak, always delivered with the right hand as the left was considered unclean. Turn the other cheek and your right-handed assailant cannot slap again but can only land a full blow, which he would only normally do to a social equal. Thus, turning the other cheek would have actually forced a relationship of either equality or non-violence with an assailant, neither of which he wants.[169]

In each case, people subvert, expose and challenge the violating power of an oppressor, using only the power that a humane and courageous faith allows them. The message of the text is that even when our neighbour's oppressive power is abundant, stable, and buttressed by authority or popular support, there are ways of subverting it while loving both self and neighbour. We are not supposed to read these as literal prescriptions for behaviour but as metaphors for creative responses to oppression; it is for us to imagine what these ancient stories mean for peace-making in the face of oppression today. The text is saying, however, that holding faith with the three fold love of God, self and neighbour is both the only authentic way to be in the world and a practical proposition in the face of oppression.

We have briefly explored how the Bible text uses metaphor to show how we might meet our oppressed or oppressive neighbour faithfully and to reassure us of the resources we need. Gandhi would later combine this wisdom with his native Hindu tradition and develop the concept of *satyagraha* (literally 'truth-force'), meaning something like 'the power of holding with truthfulness in the face of violence'. Some peace-makers today translate this as 'nonviolence', removing the hyphen to distinguish the term's associations with a transformative power from the merely negative 'non-violence', meaning simply 'not violent'. Gandhi and Martin Luther King Jr would separately build ideas like these into a method of social change, in which entire populations would seek to liberate themselves from oppression by nonviolently subverting their overlord neighbours' power.

Nonviolence in a violent world

Jesus appeared to promise that nonviolence would work. Does it? There are occasions when nonviolence leads in short order to a tangible change, such as when thousands of Egyptians refused to leave Cairo's Tahrir Square for 18 days in 2011, defying their dictator president until he stood down. Yet it would be misleading to turn this into a general rule; the worth of nonviolence is not best measured in directly cause-and-effect terms. Change comes rarely out of the blue but rather when the times are ripe for it; most work of nonviolence sets out to ripen the times. The Egyptian protests would not have been possible without smaller numbers of people working in the political darkness over many years, shaping their society's readiness for change through clandestine social action, the arts, the media and word of mouth. Through their patient work they had so ripened the times for change that when the uprising occurred in Tunisia, Egyptians did not merely watch it on TV but poured out onto the streets to change their own country in turn. The effect of Gandhi's salt march in 1930, the presence and actions of the women of Greenham Common in the 1980s, today's 'die-ins' at arms fairs, and myriad other movements has been subtly to alter the atmosphere in which societies and their leaders make choices.

The Liberian activist Leymah Gbowee helped to organise a women's sex strike as a challenge to their men to treat the violence of their country as a serious problem and to push for peace. The strike made the news because sex always does but Gbowee insists that this was just one part of the struggle with an oppressive, war-mongering male elite:

> [The] truth is that the greatest weapons of the Liberian women's movement were moral clarity, persistence, and patience. Nothing happened overnight. In fact it took three years of community awareness, sit-ins, and nonviolent demonstrations staged by ordinary "market women" – years of gathering in the roads in eye-catching white T-shirts, demanding the attention of convoys of officials and media folks who would glimpse the signs and the dancing, would hear the chanting and the singing.[170]

Now the country's former leader Charles Taylor is facing war crimes charges in The Hague. Did the women's action achieve this? It is not as simple as that, Leymah Gbowee explains:

> What we did in Liberia was to create havoc: peaceful, feminine havoc... and [now] Ellen Johnson Sirleaf leads the country. And while Liberia is still enmeshed in post-conflict strife – there have been riots in just the past few weeks – it is no longer a bloody battlefield dominated by a kind of collective insanity. Women brought sanity to Liberia.[171]

Nonviolent action is not all-powerful. Hannah Arendt argued that Gandhi's civil disobedience worked against the British state but would not have survived the far more oppressive conditions of Hitler's Germany.[172] She might be wrong – there were many missed opportunities to support German resisters in the early years of Hitler's rise to power – but she is right that applied nonviolence does not guarantee a given outcome; nothing does, violence included. Nonviolence shares with faith the same trust and doubt, the same authenticity and fallibility, and so its worth is not measured by how assured its victories are. It does not need to be perfect, just more humane and effective than violence for achieving peace, which it is. Nonviolence always gives life and in this sense, as Gandhi said, it is never a failure.

A further question mark over nonviolence is whether we are capable of the devotion it requires when faced with a brutally oppressive other. Quakers often talk about peace work as honouring that of God in every person, which means always actively seeking or listening for something of God in our neighbour. The Quaker peace worker Adam Curle described this as trying to reach the part of the other that wants to make peace with you.[173] But this is a tall order; our relationships are always bigger than we are and things go wrong. As part of a commitment to healthy relationships, sometimes things need to go awry before they can come more truly right; but at other times a neighbour has been so violent that our resources to be loving are overwhelmed. It is not then possible to love your enemies and authentic forgiveness seems out of reach, even much later.

The stories that Johann Cristoph Arnold has collected in his book *The Lost Art of Forgiving* show that the felt enormity of a past violation can put reconciliation beyond reach, yet that forgiveness is possible even for some horrific past acts of violence. Whether or not forgiveness is always ultimately possible, without it we are trapped in a life-destroying past. To move on we need forgiveness of ourselves and by ourselves, of our God and by our God, and of our neighbour and by our neighbour. Yet the slightest forcing of it makes it false. Even so, there may be no greater way to love our neighbour than to lean towards forgiveness, hope for it, ask for it and work for it.[174]

When our neighbour is neither being violated nor violating others – when neighbours greet each other as friends or as mutually curious strangers – then life flows as it should. Yet walking around London I am amazed that so many people work so hard at avoiding any connection at all of this kind, as if to shun any kind of relationship with someone they don't already know well. A genuinely good way to love our neighbour a little better is with a bit of eye contact and a "hello". It might seem trivial but in an alienated, violent world this is everyday nonviolence at work. It is apt that the English word was originally just a shout to attract another's attention. When offered and received, "hello" can reconnect two people – two fragments of society – with their mutual belonging. This small, daily peace act helps to bring us back to ourselves and creates conditions for a right, or at least better, relationship with our neighbour. It shows that peace is often made and appreciated in small ways that make a difference, as a friend of mine found:

> Just before nine this evening I popped to the corner shop. It was shut but the shopkeeper opened it up for me. We chatted. He talked about how he wanted to help me get what I needed because he doesn't like disappointing people and I thanked him. As I was leaving he said to me, I think to explain his actions, "You probably think you're the customer and I'm the one who works here but first of all we are human, aren't we."

Every day, when we genuinely connect with a neighbour, there the Kingdom of Heaven is. At one level, faith can be as simple as that.

Feeling, thinking, learning, speaking, acting

All the Samaritans of the world arrive late – the body is already bleeding in the road. The soup kitchen feeds the homeless who go on their homeless way. The humanitarian agencies ride pillion with the world's armies to tend the wounded and counsel the bereaved. All these can be authentic, humane responses to inhumanity – ways of not walking, like the priest and the Levite, "on the other side" of the road – but they all leave the violent structure of the world just as it is. The machinery of violence rolls on and somewhere on the road to Jericho thieves are beating someone up...

So love of neighbour needs also to be concerned with a commitment to the neighbourhood: acting in and for right relationship to remake a world fit for us all as neighbours. This is a commitment to social change for a more vibrant, humane society, beginning by asking what this might look like. We will not all agree on the answer but our first problem is that it is rare even to ask the question. When a drab housing estate is built, an arms deal is struck, and punishment is nine tenths of criminal justice, the question of whether this is leading towards a vibrant, humane society is not in the field. A continuous conversation is needed in society about the kinds of communities – local and global – we are creating and the values they reflect.

Re-creating the neighbourhood means reconfiguring the structures that govern power, so that when exercised it facilitates our common being rather than oppresses it. This inevitably means working to transform the political and economic systems that determine how power is shared and used. A hope of peace is that these structures – from those of a family or faith community to the forces shaping our lives at a global level – come to reflect a shared feeling for what is most valuable, or sacred, about being alive. To this end, the work is of perhaps four broad kinds:

+ dismantling structures of violence, such as militarism, unjust economics, consumerism;
+ redeeming structures that may be 'fallen', such as democratic systems, local economies/community spaces, education, faith traditions;
+ preserving structures that give life, such as the natural world, human rights and freedoms, the arts;
+ creating new life-giving structures, such as peace and solidarity networks, intentional communities and community-building initiatives.

Structures are social, economic, political and ecological, as well as the cultures of thinking and behaviour on which they depend. The sphere of peace-making is therefore the whole of life and society. Discerning what and how to give will involve all people of a peace-making faith appraising all the skills, resources and passions available. Consider the arts, which at their best can unsettle, inspire, reveal, startle, renew or in some other way bring us more fully to life in the world. Like faith, the arts can bring us back to a feeling for what life is really about, without which nonviolence would die. Like the nonviolent direct activist, the world-aware artist can shake us awake to the world as it is, challenge us to respond, and support and inspire us in the process; activist and artist both have their place in a movement of peace-making.

Similarly, a commitment to peace means recognising that everything we imagine ourselves to possess – our minds, bodies, buildings, skills, interests, passions, time, labour and so on – is a potential resource for peace-making. If we are truly given to peace-making, then we will understand our resources also to be given, including our money. Of course, our money is still our own insofar as we choose how to use it, but in another sense it belongs in the service of what is sacred and comes before us in the universe. Again, the surplus resource is not for hoarding but for returning to where it is needed; we cannot give more than we are able to offer, but insofar as we are faithful we can give no less, either. Most Quaker groups have meeting houses; are they sitting empty during the week or are they fully pressed into the service of peace?

By thinking creatively about what is possible, often very simple offerings count. This is Caroline Westgate's description of a disarmament action:

> On Monday this week there was another big blockade at Faslane. For six hours about eight hundred people nonviolently prevented any vehicles or personnel from entering or leaving the base where the [Trident] submarines are berthed and serviced. Three hundred and fifty people were arrested ... I walked around with my one-woman "Quakers for Peace" banner and handed out industrial quantities of vegan flapjack – a few extra calories for people who had been awake since five in the morning and who still had a lot of day to get through…[175]

While Caroline is handing out the flapjack, other people are making sure everyone has water, others are acting as minibus drivers, musicians or legal observers for the expected court case, liaising with the police, praying and giving thanks, and a few are lying in the road across the gate holding a space for what some of us call the Kingdom of Heaven, waiting for arrest. Everyone is participating, everyone has something to offer, and in offering it everything stands up for life and peace in a small way that counts. Caroline's action plays its part in the long, slow *metanoia* process to abolish the violence of Trident.

The Quaker Chuck Fager notes the military term "tooth-to-tail", the ratio of front-line combat troops to the much greater numbers in support, and he encourages peace activists to think in the same way.[176] Everyone on the front line of peace work, and there are many ways of understanding what that means, needs a community of support and we can all be part of it. After all, making flapjack is not difficult; Caroline has the recipe.

As the Trident Ploughshares movement demonstrates, taking part in the social conversation about the kind of society we want to live in is not usually a matter of sitting around a table with the powers that be. It happens in the world; the speaking and listening are done through how lives are lived and held together in a common commitment. When in faith we feel, think, learn, speak, act, we participate in the conversation of our society; sometimes creating a dialogue where one did not exist before, sometimes insisting on one with people in power who would rather we went home. The letter on disarmament to the MP, the nonviolent direct action or the poetry reading in the park does not itself beat swords into ploughshares. It does engage the world in life-giving questions that have been ignored and helps to ripen the times for a society committed to a shared feeling for what matters most. This comes first from a commitment, or witness, to the dignity of our being – no matter what – and this makes it different from pitching up at a demonstration once in a while and then losing interest when nothing seems to change. "Call it 'militant gradualism'", writes the criminal justice academic Mike Nellis,

> … [for] in truth, if culture can't be changed by diktat from above (and it can't), what else is there but this piecemeal, ground-level approach? What other means are available to ordinary non-violent people who do what they do for love and nothing, in their spare time?[177]

And so a commitment to peace will take us away from the quiet life, not towards it. It will nonviolently breach the 'peace' – not the vibrant, flourishing peace of *shalom* but the fettered, lifeless *pax* of what Herbert Marcuse called the "comfortable, smooth, reasonable, democratic unfreedom" of industrialised society.[178] Just as Jesus disturbed the *Pax Romana* and Gandhi the *Pax Britannica*, so a commitment to peace now will disturb the *Pax Alienata* of the modern world. As I understand it, this is what Quakers and others are trying to do, including through nonviolent direct action at such centres of violence as Faslane.

The shared courage and imagination needed to move into a more alive, disturbing way of being can and does change the world. Writing about what made the Velvet Revolution in Czechoslovakia possible, Václav Havel cannot credit a particular epiphany, act of extraordinary heroism or stroke of good fortune. The change that Charter 77 helped to bring about happened in a "hidden sphere", he says.[179] Similarly most peace work is groundwork, in which many tiny changes in a hidden sphere slowly turn impossibilities into possibilities. The seasoned anti-nuclear campaigner Rebecca Johnson likens the institution of nuclear weapons to a huge rock on a mountain-top. One day it will fall, she says, because thousands of people have been digging away at its foundations with spoons and eventually there will be nothing left to hold it up.[180] It is as if one day the big change that everyone said was unrealistic – abolition of slavery, abolition of capital punishment, civil partnerships, the fall of the Wall, nuclear disarmament – is revealed as the rational option it always was, as if out of the blue. So we hope.

None of this is possible unless we can connect and keep reconnecting with a peace-making community, its shared sense of what matters most, and those surprising promptings of love and truth that push up, mushroom-like, through the tarmac-crust of the everyday. By these promptings we know our sun, centre of gravity and source for a community devoted to the dignity of being. If there is a single plea in this book it is that our faith may shape us into such communities as these, that we may know experimentally and act adventurously, openly, curiously and with a passion for being alive that is shared and shared again.

7

Starting again

The Quaker peace testimony is not a right-thinking ideology about the moral error of violence; it is the practical working-out of a heart-and-soul commitment to live within, and create, right relationships in a violent world. This is what holding faith with life – trying to be a 'people of God' – is involving the Quaker movement in, or so we might hope. This commitment brings us into a conflict with how we are living and how society is structured; by facing up to that conflict we change and so does the world. But if the change within us has not yet begun – if we do not identify with being 'shaken' and if the long turn of *metanoia* means nothing to us – then nothing in this will make sense. This is what William Penn was driving at when he described the earliest Quakers:

> They were changed men themselves before they went about to change others. Their hearts were rent as well as their garments; and they knew the power and work of God upon them.[181]

This last chapter is about how a commitment to peace settled in the minds and hearts of the founders of the Quaker movement and what we can take from that story today. Its backdrop is the startlingly different world of the mid-seventeenth century, which nonetheless shows striking parallels with our situation now.

"Conversation in the world"

The early Quakers were born into history amid the tumult of great social, political and spiritual upheaval. The established church, to which people had looked as a singular spiritual compass in a way that is difficult to imagine today, had become preoccupied with its own authority, alienated from the people and the life-giving message of the Gospel. King and parliament vied for state power, and as a new market economy began to consolidate farmland and create larger industries, the gap between rich and poor was widening. People were feeling oppressed spiritually and politically and society seemed to have lost its way.

As the Quaker historian John Punshon points out, most people probably kept their heads down and carried on as best they could, but many did not.[182] With the old certainties now in question, new political and religious space opened and excited a new idealism. The crisis spurred many to imagine a better society and give themselves over to working for it.

A motley clutch of movements formed to challenge established authority, many with egalitarian ideals such as the Levellers and the Diggers. Such dissenting movements were 'the shaken' of their times. With the English translation of the Bible now available, people could interpret its meaning according to their own situation without the dubious help of a priestly class with its vested interests. New movements were finding new ways to interpret the Christian story; many believed they were uncovering an older, more authentic and politically radical Christianity that had been lost. Some of the religious groups that preceded Quakers were already experimenting with silent worship, nonviolence, egalitarianism and personal experience of the divine. Many read the collapsing social order as a signal for the coming divine judgement at the end of time, and were confident that their brand of faithfulness would help to fulfil God's work in the world. Quakers were one such group.

The new movements spelt trouble for church and state, which moved to quell them. Before the Quaker movement was a decade old it was facing persecution, culminating in the preventive arrest of four thousand Friends in 1660. In early 1661 a group of 12 Quakers submitted *A Declaration from the Harmless and Innocent People of God called Quakers* to the newly crowned Charles II, pleading with him to release their brethren. The document complained that Quakers were being "...beaten, stoned, wounded, stocked, whipped, imprisoned, haled out of synagogues, cast into dungeons and noisome vaults where many [had] died in bonds..." Its authors sought to reassure the king that Quakers presented no threat to his rule and so he had nothing to fear from allowing them to live in peace.

In distancing Quakers not only from violence but from all political struggle the document can be read as self-serving and inappropriately neutral, but this is a tough judgement. Quakers outside prison had both to be faithful to their own convictions and to make a persuasive case to the king on behalf of their incarcerated friends. The *Declaration* was intended to serve this purpose and it needs to be read in that way, although it is also more radical than it might at first appear.

At this time Quakers did not form a broadly united, ordered body. Without meetings of representatives or an agreed set of practices, they relied on a loosely shared sense of their truth, powered by personal inspiration and spread by word of mouth. The *Declaration* could not therefore speak for all Quakers, but it was an early example of a commonly discerned – and contested – statement of their approach to the world. It shows how Friends' visceral feeling for their truth began to settle into discrete ideas and convictions. Besides the negative assurance that Quakers intended the king no harm, the document makes clear for the first time their commitment to a non-violent revolution based on changes in the hearts and minds of people.

Until this point Quakers did not generally identify with a commitment to non-violence. The historian David Boulton shows that in the 1650s, many – perhaps most – Quakers believed the New Model Army was doing God's work, and many fought in it.[183] Even so, there were exceptions and amid the violence of the time there were at least suggestions of an emerging, theologically grounded, commitment to peace. Whether the *Declaration* marks a natural evolution towards a peace commitment, a politically convenient U-turn or, most likely, both, the document attempts to settle the matter from that point forward. Alluding to the Apostle Paul, it says that Quakers' "conversation in the world" – that is, their revolutionary aspirations – was now of a non-violent kind.[184] They would later call this revolutionary process their "peace testimony".

"Weapons must be spiritual"

The worldview of Quakers and other religious radicals was that we all live in two worlds at once. The first world is the redeemed world of the spiritually ordered community with God at its centre. The other is the fallen, imploding world of everyday affairs: political corruption, social strife, greed and the rest, dragging itself down into its own maelstrom. Some dissenters were happy to be redeemed privately while the violent, fallen world fell ever further. The radicals, however, saw the two worlds as locked in a struggle on which the future of everything hung; a battle between faithfulness and fallenness was under way in the world.

Many dissenters looked to political struggle, sometimes of a violent kind, to bring freedom to the people in Christ's name. Quakers went a different way. They believed the struggle between the two worlds was being waged on the battlefield of everyone's heart, torn as they were between the living impulses of "the Truth" that came from God – that is, a feeling for what is sacred – and the dead values of the fallen, everyday world.

Several years before the *Declaration*, William Dewsbury, then not a Quaker, was fighting in the New Model Army "in obedience to my God".[185] There he had an epiphany, realising that his war with his enemy was false. The authentic struggle between the redeemed world of God and the fallen world of human hubris was going on within Dewsbury's own soul (and within his supposed enemy's soul, too, whether or not he realised it). As Dewsbury put it, he saw then that

> the Kingdom of Christ was within, and the enemies was within, and was spiritual, and my weapons against them must be spiritual, the power of God.[186]

Herein lay "the mystery of iniquity", he wrote – the spiritual failure that accounts for why the world is a fallen and violent place. Having identified this as the authentic struggle of his faith, he could "no longer fight with a carnal weapon against a carnal man".[187]

This religious language is heady stuff by today's standards and possibly off-putting for those of us who do not look to the Christian story to frame all of human experience. If we try to enter into the worldview of the time, however, we can see that William Dewsbury had an insight into the deep structure of violence and redemption: that 'good' and 'evil' are not the same as 'us' and 'them'. When we think they are, violence is on the way. Dewsbury's mortal quarrel could not be with his neighbour, therefore, but with the forces in his neighbour and himself that led them to try to kill each other.

Curiously, a version of this insight is reflected in one of the psychological defences of Freudian theories of the mind, called splitting.[188] In order not to be psychologically overwhelmed by the complexities of good and evil, we split them between, for example, a good mother and evil father, friend and foe, Christianity and Islam, Labour and Conservative, me and my enemy, and so on. We do this, the theory goes, because it is psychologically demanding to recognise that we are not entirely righteous and our 'enemy' is not entirely evil – too demanding for some of our newspapers, for example. The effect of Dewsbury's epiphany is to humanise his 'enemy' – to see him as a complex being in the same spiritually oppressed condition as everyone else.

So for early Quakers like Dewsbury, violence could not be a tool to wield against sin because it was sin; God's struggle, in contrast, was against the broken spiritual condition that was leading the world into violence. Another early Quaker, James Nayler, followed Dewsbury by identifying this spiritual labour with that of Jesus, the "Lamb of God" at work in the world. In the following extract, thick as it is with symbolism, "the creature" means a person as a created, and therefore fallen, being:

> The Lamb's quarrel is not against the creation [i.e. against people], for then should his weapons be carnal, as the weapons of the worldly spirits [i.e. governments and factions] are: "For we war not with flesh and blood," nor against the creation of God; that we love; but we fight against the spiritual powers of wickedness, which wars against God in the creation, and captivates the creation into the lust which wars against the soul, and [we fight so] that the creature may be delivered into its liberty...[189]

STARTING AGAIN | 119

Like William Dewsbury, James Nayler understood that beneath a violent system or choice is a spiritual failure of a sort that has "captivated" the world. If we transform that part of us that is tempted into violence then – and only then – can we "be delivered into ... liberty". Again, the antagonist who stands against us is not our real enemy because God's "quarrel", and therefore ours as a people following God, is not with people but with our common fallenness.

The *Declaration* follows these earlier epiphanies by referencing a passage from the Letter of James, which forms the theological cornerstone of the early Quakers' critique of violence. In the King James Bible that Quakers used, the text reads:

> From whence come wars and fighting among you? Come they not hence, even of your lusts that war in your members? Ye lust, and have not: ye kill, and desire to have, and cannot obtain: ye fight and war, yet ye have not, because ye ask not. Ye ask, and receive not, because ye ask amiss, that ye may consume it upon your lusts.[190]

"Lusts" means all desires and judgements that are not of God. Quakers took this to mean that we are violent because we have allowed our lives to be ruled by desires that are, in the language of a later age, alienated from God and our neighbour. James was saying that when we indulge our hubris in the belief that it is ours to impose our own order on the cosmos, ours to take what has not been given and ours to profess more than we actually know, violence is inevitable. So James' message is not merely that we fight because we are selfish, in the sense of being preoccupied with our own interests to the exclusion of others. Rather, the desires that lead us to fight for political power, even when we think this is for God's sake, are of a kind that puts ourselves, and not God, at the centre of the world. Only by seeking God first and "asking" – and not asking "amiss" but really listening for an answer and then serving it – can the Kingdom of God take hold in the world. The repudiation of 'plottings' against the king was not only politically pragmatic for Quakers in 1661 but also grounded in theological principle.

The *Declaration* claims that in following God, Quakers would never violate another person with "outward weapons, neither for the kingdom of Christ [i.e. for God's revolutionary purposes in the world] nor for the kingdoms of this world [i.e. for political power]." Those who thought they could build the Kingdom of Heaven through violence betrayed both the Kingdom and themselves in doing so. Quakers believed, and still do today, that God's work could never be achieved by violating other people, however noble the aims of such violence might be.

"Seek peace and ensue it"

Having renounced violence, the *Declaration* goes on to explain the sort of non-violent revolution that its authors were encouraging all to join. Rather than allowing our "lusts" to make violent beings of us, the revolution begins with listening for what Isaac Penington would later call a "present sense" of the Holy Spirit working through our lives. This "present sense" consists in what many Quakers today describe as spiritually listening for the "promptings of Love and Truth in your hearts".[191] For early Friends this practice reflected a theology of the resurrection: Christ had died on the cross and then risen within the hearts of the people of God – the people that Quakers felt themselves to be. But this theology was for all comers: whatever their religious persuasion, anyone could find God in a present sense of Love and Truth, and so join the revolution.

By being faithful to their truth, Quakers found that their "captivated" selves could loosen their bonds; their hearts drew "…into love and unity with God…" and so were "redeemed" but it was a daily struggle.[192] There is more than a little Puritan influence in this characterisation of faithfulness as a constant battle with sin. Quaker meetings were often several hours long and if a worshipper succumbed to anything as worldly as a snooze a special long pole was sometimes employed to waken them again to their Christian discipline. Be that as it may, Quakers were can-do spiritual optimists, too. The *Declaration* clearly implies that only a right relationship with God or, to put it another way, a feeling for what is sacred, turns us to a right relationship with each other. As this process develops, people are lifted out of the "occasion of war" (where 'occasion' has a now-obsolete sense, meaning 'reason for' or 'motivation to').[193] Now redeemed from war-making, says the text, Quaker practice would always "seek peace and ensue it, … seeking the good and welfare and doing that which tends to the peace of all".[194]

The *Declaration* says that as God enters the world through the hearts of the faithful and overcomes their self-interested desires, a spiritually ordered community establishes itself like a pocket of the Kingdom of God right inside a violent, fallen world. Quakers did not agree with many other Christians who believed that the Kingdom of God was a supernatural place or an event at the end of time. Rather, the Kingdom of God was made real in the world once the true or sacred was allowed its place at the centre of lives and communities. Quakers thought – wrongly as it happened – that as the Kingdom burgeoned with every newly redeemed person, this collective *metanoia* would in short order transform the whole world. This is the revolution that these supposedly "harmless" people were commending to King Charles. As they put it:

> …we do earnestly desire and wait, that by the Word of God's power and its effectual operation in the hearts of men, the kingdoms of this world may become the kingdoms of the Lord, and of his Christ, that he may

rule and reign in men by his spirit and truth, that thereby all people, out of all different judgements and professions may be brought into love and unity with God, and one with another, and that they may all come to witness the prophet's words who said, "Nation shall not lift up sword against nation, neither shall they learn war any more."[195]

All that flows from this spiritual transformation is what the *Declaration* calls Friends' 'testimony' to the world, following the biblical meaning of an embodied truth. The outward sign of this truth is to be "doing that which tends to the peace of all", reflecting the interior reality of a people "brought into love and unity with God", or in other words a God-centred community. This revolution was to be fought with spiritual "weapons", empowered by a present sense of God at work in Quakers and in the world.

The possibility of experiencing God directly already had a long history in the Jewish *midrash* tradition and earlier Christian monastic practices.[196] At the time of early Friends' persecutions, however, the idea that personal and collective experience could reinterpret received religious truths was spiritually radical and politically dangerous. Quakers contrasted their experiential approach to religion with the church authorities, which Isaac Penington criticised as mired in a merely notional understanding of faith. Its clergy were just going through the motions, observing but not feeling, he believed, for

…they know not indeed Christ in his nature, Spirit, life, and power; because they speak not of him as persons who feel the thing, and speak from the present sense of it, and acquaintance with it, but only as persons that bring forth a notion they have received into their understandings.[197]

For Quakers, the main space in which a "present sense" of God could be encountered was a meeting for worship – that is, a gathered community expectantly awaiting the presence of God – as well as in a sense of what is sacred in everyday life. Quakers did not believe themselves to be inventing a new Christianity, but rediscovering the lost discipleship of the early church, in which a committed community of people followed in the path of Jesus and really meant it.

However, Quakers' emphasis on personal experience was not a licence to reduce religion to a private, anything-goes spirituality outside the discourse of their faith tradition. The early Quaker leadership certainly knew the Bible very well and used it constantly not only to confound their detractors but to inspire, authorise and develop their own spiritual convictions. Indeed, they were steeped in the debates and enquiries that the priestly class had engaged in for centuries, such as the doctrine of the Trinity and the divine nature of Jesus.

Holy Experiment

The *Declaration* failed to stop the persecution by church and state but unknown numbers of Quakers and other dissenters refused to be cowed and continued to worship in their own ways. Even being bundled off to prison or transported appeared an impotent punishment for those who continued their worship wherever they could. If you visit Lancaster Castle today you can be treated to a few seconds in one of its seventeenth-century prison cells; these underground dungeons have mud floors, no sanitation and, once the museum guide has closed you in with 20 or so others, no earthly light at all. A few seconds are more than enough.

When the world was not overcome by the spirit of Christ and God did not end it all with a final judgement, Quakers began to see their work as an open-ended, experimental commitment to peace. They began to realise that spiritual revolution went hand in hand with social change; not only should Quakers live as if the Kingdom of God were already in their hearts, but should testify to the same truth in the world by trying to make society fit for such changed and changing hearts.

This led to all manner of spiritually inspired works in the kinds of fallen, 'worldly' contexts that Quakers had earlier avoided. William Penn went on to found Pennsylvania on the world's first declaration of fundamental freedoms. He called this new society a "Holy Experiment", hoping that the ideals of peace might be realised there, and for some time they largely were. Penn's pamphlet calling on European nations to come together in peace by setting up a common parliament still inspires Europeans today.[198] As William Penn's work shows, early Friends were religiously ardent but their fervour was gradually tempered and grounded by a simple common-sense humanity as a people of practical hope. With no end to violence in sight, Quaker hopes rested then as now on the simple politics of lives transformed through faithfulness, coupled with work to evolve societies into less violent, more humane places to be.

In the same tradition Quakers have continued to work for peace, justice and relief of suffering. From the statesmanship of William Penn in the seventeenth century, to the anti-slavery work of John Woolman and others in the eighteenth, to the philanthropy, poverty relief and prison reform in the nineteenth, to the international humanitarian relief, conscientious objection and anti-militarism in the twentieth, Quakers have sustained a lively peace-making tradition, albeit with many ups and downs.

In the last 50 years or so, the scope of Quaker testimony has broadened with the mushrooming of concerns and interests: criminal justice, housing, social diversity, civil and human rights, economic reform and development, the democratic system, the spiritual growth of young people, mediation, ecological awareness and responsibility, ecumenical and interfaith relations, applied nonviolence, interpersonal conflict and business ethics, to name but a few. All in their small but significant way help to grow the peace of *shalom* and challenge the multiple violations of violence from the local level to the global. The Quaker community broadly owns its contribution to this work by means of an elaborate, sometimes perplexing, network of committees that help to ensure that everyone is involved.

A strength of the Quaker movement is a willingness to pioneer new ideas, particularly unpopular ones such as the current work in Britain to provide small communities of support and accountability for released sex offenders. Another is a willingness to be facilitators – impartial brokers, go-betweens and builders of movements – without insisting on having the Quaker logo included. Quakers' historic strengths as pioneers and facilitators have created and sustained peace-making initiatives long after many others (but not all) have gone home.

"School for peacemakers"

Quakers are still cultivating that slow revolution of the heart while working in many small ways for the same in the great neighbourhood of the Earth. At the same time, many individual Quaker activists are frustrated that some of their fellows show little interest in the challenging and unsettling vocation of being a radical movement of change or a radically loving community. Instead, other concerns take precedence – does the community have enough money, is it big enough, is it sufficiently well known? In this climate, Sunday morning worship is reduced to a haven for individual meditation away from the world, and the community starts to measure its progress according to whether it is growing or shrinking in number rather than how faithful it is. It is understandable that the prospect of faith as discipleship

– that is, as something disturbing – can be scary. Nonetheless, as a people of faith Quakers are not an escape route from a violent world, but are called to incarnate love within it.

This is not to criticise Quakers and other faith communities as not good enough – there are too many 'not good enough' messages in the world already – but to ask what they are becoming. Is the alienation of modern life domesticating our faith traditions or radicalising them into the centres of peace-making that they need to be and for which their founders hoped? Really loving our own faith communities means treating them as worthy of becoming a people of God; that is, a people who are both comforted and challenged by faith, testifying to its truth through work in the world. This means first wanting to be communities that are, as Sandra Cronk wrote, "a school for peacemakers", in which "God's gift of peace is learned, practiced, and nurtured".[199] In such a community, everyone is supported and challenged to play their part.

Today the hearts of Quakers, and perhaps of all, are as torn as they ever have been between a life-giving world of 'God', whatever we conceive God to be, and a fallen world of violence and alienation. To borrow the language of early Quakers, in the gospel world faithfulness is sufficient unto itself, caring only to be truthful and not about what name it is given or how big its community is or how much money it has. But we are all of the other world also, in which a people of God becomes accommodated to secular preoccupations. Then, a life of faith is seen not as the only realistic one possible in a world such as ours, but as naïve – something to be interested in, perhaps, but not to be in.

The world of *shalom* is, as ever, in trouble, and now we face possibly the most serious crisis in history: a pervasively violent world combined with the threat of ecological collapse. The word crisis has two meanings: a moment of great difficulty and a moment requiring urgent decision. At this time of difficulty and decision it matters whether the way we are living and organising our societies flows from what we feel, in our deepest selves, life is really about. It matters that we ask what it means in today's world to live and commune faithfully – with all the personal, political and spiritual resonances that word has. And it matters whether we can create communities capable of working for a world of vibrant and humane relationships: communities resistant to the forces that alienate us from ourselves, one another and the Earth. Is this not a holy experiment worthy of our day?

A week after the atrocities of 11 September 2001 Alfred Moon, a Quaker from Uxbridge Meeting, called me at the Peace & Disarmament desk in Friends House to ask what Quakers were doing for peace and what he could do. We both knew that the bombing of Afghanistan would soon start. As we talked I remarked glibly that the attacks had set back the Kingdom of Heaven a few years. "The Kingdom of Heaven is now," he said.

Thanks

Thanks to Sam Walton and the Peace Campaigning and Networking Group of Quaker Peace & Social Witness for asking me to write this book; and to Philip Austin, Jonathan Baxter, Cecile Brich, Hubert Cassel, Sarah Gittins, Ingrid Mackay, Kristen Neumann-Martiensen, Deborah Padfield and Steve Whiting for their encouragement and thoughtful comments on a draft. Special thanks to Mary Lou Leavitt, Sunniva Taylor and Louisa Wright for having the patience to read successive drafts and never let me off the hook. I would also like to thank Sarah Gittins for allowing Quaker Books to use her work, Pale Blue Window, on the cover; Kaye Lee for her poem, Beyond; and John Lynes for checking that I was representing his experience appropriately. Finally, I thank the Quaker movement for its support and teaching, and for still promising to be a community that changes the world.

Endnotes

[1] Extrapolated from Forbes 'The world's billionaires', http://www.forbes. com/wealth/billionaires/list, accessed 13 March 2011, and United Nations Development Programme, *Human development report 2010: The real wealth of nations – pathways to human development* (New York. UNDP, 2010), pp. 8, 96. Poorest 1.44bn people earn no more than $1.25 a day and a further 1.16bn earn no more than $2 a day; based on global population of 6.8 billion.

[2] Northern Friends Peace Board, *The peace papers* (Bolton: NFPB, 2000–2002).

[3] W. Brueggemann, *The prophetic imagination* (n.p.: Fortress Press, 1978).

[4] Charter 77, 'Declaration of CHARTER '77', http://libpro.cts.cuni. cz/charta/docs/declaration_of_charter_77.pdf?q=jelent, accessed 9 November 2010.

[5] J. Patočka, in A. Shanks, *God and modernity: A new and better way to do theology* (London: Routledge, 2000), p. 5.

[6] A. Shanks, *God and modernity*, p. 4.

[7] J. Patočka, in Shanks, *God and modernity*, p. 5.

[8] A. Rose, 'Violence/non-violence' in Dale, J., *Faith in action: Quaker social testimony* (London: Quaker Home Service, 2000).

[9] B. Okri, *A way of being free* (London: Phoenix, 1997), pp. 13–14.

[10] Richard Dawkins Foundation for Reason and Science, http://richarddawkins.net, accessed 16 September 2010.

[11] W. James, 'The will to believe' (1896), James Madison University website, http://falcon.jmu.edu/~omearawm/ph101willtobelieve.html, accessed 22 July 2010.

[12] I. Crichton Smith (1986) in A. McIntosh, *Hell and high water: Climate change, hope and the human condition* (Edinburgh: Birlinn, 2008), p. 154.

[13] R. Williams, 'Apostles and prophets: Can we speak for God?' [audio presentation given at Greenbelt Christian Arts Festival], 2004.

[14] K. Armstrong, *The Bible: The biography* (Croydon: Atlantic, 2007), p. 117.

[15] P. V. Rajagopal (2010) Talk to QPSW Annual Conference, Derbyshire.

[16] I. C. Heyward, *The redemption of God: A theology of mutual relation* (Lanham, MD: University Press of America, 1982), p. 9.

[17] M. Gandhi (1984) in T. Merton, ed., *Gandhi on non-violence.* (London: Shambala, 1996), p. 150.

[18] Faith and Order Team, World Council of Churches, *Nurturing peace, overcoming violence: In the way of Christ for the sake of the world* (Geneva: WCC, 2002), p. 4.

[19] W. Brueggemann, *The prophetic imagination* (n.p.: Fortress Press, 1978).

[20] John (14:27).

[21] D. Ford, *Theology: A very short introduction* (Oxford: Oxford University Press, 1999), pp. 7–11.

[22] Gospel of Thomas, Saying 2, http://www.gospelthomas.com, accessed 19 December 2004.

[23] H. Steven (1984) in Yearly Meeting of the Religious Society of Friends (Quakers) in Britain, *Quaker faith & practice (4th edn).* (London: Yearly Meeting of the Religious Society of Friends (Quakers) in Britain, 2009), 24.27.

[24] J. Patočka, (1975) in Shanks, *God and modernity,* pp. 4–5.

[25] M. Longley, (2011) [Poetry reading, 2 March].

[26] Okri, *A way of being free,* pp. 111.

[27] J. Macy, *World as lover, world as self* (Berkeley: Parallax, 1991), p. 185.

28 'Terry' (2010) [personal communication].

29 D. K. Gibran, *The Falklands War: Britain versus the past in the South Atlantic* (Jefferson: McFarland, 1998), p. 133.

30 M. Middlebrook, *Task force: The Falklands War 1982* (revised edn) (London: Penguin, 1987).

31 BBC News, 'UK "regret" over Falklands dead' (1 April 2007), http://news.bbc.co.uk/1/hi/uk/6515803.stm, accessed 8 November 2010.

32 V. Bramley in D. Hallock, *Bloody hell: The price soldiers pay* (Robertsbridge: Plough, 1999), p. 65.

33 World Health Organisation, *World report on violence and health* (Geneva: WHO, 2002), p. 5.

34 Ibid., p. 218.

35 Ibid., p. 218.

36 Ibid., p. 223.

37 N. Fear et al., 'What are the consequences of deployment to Iraq and Afghanistan on the mental health of the UK armed forces? A cohort study' (13 May 2010), The Lancet website, http://www.thelancet.com/journals/lancet/article/PIIS0140-6736(10)60672-1/fulltext, accessed 13 May 2010; S. McManus et al., eds., 'Adult psychiatric morbidity in England, 2007: Results of a household survey', The NHS Information Centre website, http://www.ic.nhs.uk/pubs/psychiatricmorbidity07, accessed 13 May 2010.

38 C. W. Hoge, et al., 'Combat duty in Iraq and Afghanistan, mental health problems, and barriers to care' in *The New England Journal of Medicine*, 351 (2004), pp. 13–22.

39 United Nations, *Charter of the United Nations*, 1945, ch. V.

40 Stockholm International Peace Research Institute, 'The 15 countries with the highest military expenditure in 2009', http://www.sipri.org/research/armaments/milex/resultoutput/milex_15, accessed 16 August 2010; A. Shah, 'The arms trade is big business', Global Issues website, http://www.globalissues.org/article/74/the-arms-trade-is-big-business, accessed 27 August 2010.

41 J. Smith and T. Smith, 'Nuclear war: The medical facts' in *BMJ*, 283 (1981), pp. 771–774.

[42] P. Cawson et al., *Child maltreatment in the United Kingdom: A study of the prevalence of child abuse and neglect* (London: NSPCC, 2000), p.83, p.85, p.89.

[43] L. Kelly et al., 'A gap or a chasm? Attrition in reported rape cases' (Home Office Research Study 293) in NSPCC, *Child sexual abuse: Key child protection statistics*. (London: NSPCC, 2007), p. 26.

[44] Cawson et al,. *Child maltreatment in the United Kingdom*, p. 35; D. Povey, D et al., *Homicides, firearms offences and intimate violence 2006/2007: Supplementary volume 2 to Crime in England and Wales 2006/2007*, cited in 'Babies and toddlers at risk', NSPCC website, http://www.nspcc.org.uk/Inform/research/statistics/babies_and_toddlers_at_risk_statistics_wda48732.html, accessed 18 November 2010.

[45] Department of Health (2002) in Women's Aid, 'Domestic violence: Frequently asked questions' and 'Statistics: Domestic violence', www.womensaid.org.uk, accessed 16 August 2010.

[46] World Health Organisation, *World report on violence and health*, p. 33.

[47] NSPCC, *Child sexual abuse: Key child protection statistics* (London: NSPCC, 2007).

[48] World Health Organisation, *World report on violence and health*, p. 27.

[49] K. Hawton et al., 'Deliberate self harm in adolescents: Self report survey in schools in England' in *BMJ*, 325 (2002), p. 1207.

[50] Home Office, *Crime in England and Wales 2009/10: Findings from the British Crime Survey and police recorded crime* (2nd edn) (London: Home Office, 2010), p. 72. 21% of both sexes abused since age 16; 5% in the last year.

[51] S. Walby, and J. Allen, *Domestic violence, sexual assault and stalking: Findings from the British Crime Survey* (London: Home Office, 2004), p. v–xi.

[52] Zero Tolerance Charitable Trust, cited in Women's Aid, 'Statistics: Domestic violence', www.womensaid.org.uk, accessed 16 August 2010.

[53] J. Gilligan, *Violence: Reflections on a national epidemic* (New York: Vintage, 1997), p. 194.

[54] P. Farmer (1997), 'On suffering and structural violence: A view from below' in N. Scheper-Hughes, and P. Bourgois, eds., *Violence in war and peace: An anthology* (Oxford: Blackwell, 2004) p. 288.

[55] Extrapolated from World Health Organisation, *World report on violence and health*, p. 286.

[56] FAO (2009) in World Hunger Education Service, 'World hunger and poverty facts and statistics 2010'. http://www.worldhunger.org/articles/Learn/world%20hunger%20facts%202002.htm, accessed 22 October 2010.

[57] United Nations Inter-agency Group for Child Mortality Estimation, *Levels & trends in child mortality: Report 2010* (New York: Unicef, 2010), p. 1.

[58] Ibid., p. 10.

[59] R. Wilkinson and K. Pickett, *The spirit level: Why equality is better for everyone* (London: Penguin, 2010), p. 284. $r > 0.4$ and $p < 0.05$ for each social problem, $r = 0.87$ and $p < 0.01$ for index of all problems, equally weighted.

[60] Wilkinson and Pickett, *The spirit level*, p. 240; M. Shaw, et al., 'Health inequalities and New Labour: How the promises compare with real progress' in *BMJ*, 330 (2005), p. 1019. Appendix (for web only) at http://www.bmj.com/content/330/7498/1016/suppl/DC1, accessed 23 October 2010.

[61] Wilkinson and Pickett, *The spirit level*, p. 15; World Health Organisation (2008:32); M. Shaw, et al., 'Health inequalities and New Labour', appendix.

[62] I. Crichton Smith, 'Real people in a real place' in *Towards the human* (Loanhead: Macdonald, 1986).

[63] International Soil Reference and Information Centre, *Global survey of human-induced soil degradation*, cited in 'Land degradation', University of Michigan Global Change Program website, http://www.globalchange.umich.edu/globalchange2/current/lectures/land_deg/land_deg.html, accessed 22 September 2010.

[64] Millennium Ecosystem Assessment Secretariat, *Millennium ecosystems and human well-being: Current state and trends*, volume 1, (Washington DC: Island Press, 2005), p. 79.

[65] International Soil Reference and Information Centre, *Global survey of human-induced soil degradation*; N. Stern, *The Stern review on the economics of climate change* (London: The Stationery Office, 2006), p. iv; Millennium Ecosystem Assessment Secretariat, *Millennium ecosystems and human well-being*, p. 79.

[66] R. Betts, 'Four degrees and beyond' (28 September 2009), Met Office website, http://www.metoffice.gov.uk/climatechange/news/latest/four-degrees.html, accessed 22 September 2010.

[67] Stern, *The Stern review on the economics of climate change*, p. v.

[68] Ibid., p. v.

[69] Ibid., p. vi.

[70] Ibid., p. v.

[71] Quaker Council for European Affairs, *EU sustainable consumption and production action plan: Briefing, evaluation, and action for Quakers* (Brussels: QCEA, 2010), p. 9 (includes emissions from trade); data also extrapolated from various sources including DECC *et al* (2009); Research and Markets, 'Clothing & footwear industry market review 2010', http://www.researchandmarkets.com/reportinfo.asp?report_id=1288211, accessed 6 October 2010; G. Lean, 'Cow "emissions" more damaging to planet than CO2 from cars' (10 December 2006), The Independent website, http://www.independent.co.uk/environment/climate-change/cow-emissions-more-damaging-to-planet-than-cosub2sub-from-cars-427843.html, accessed 6 October 2010, and others.

[72] R. Pachauri, 'Speech by Dr Rajendra Pachauri' (7 December 2009), United Nations Framework Convention on Climate Change website, http://unfccc.int/files/meetings/cop_15/statements/application/pdf/rkp-welc-cer-cop15.pdf, accessed 22 September 2010.

[73] Stockholm International Peace Research Institute, 'The 15 countries with the highest military expenditure in 2009'.

[74] R. Pachauri, 'Speech by Dr Rajendra Pachauri'.

[75] P. Baer et al., *The greenhouse development rights framework: The right to development in a climate constrained world* (Berlin: Heinrich-Böll-Stiftung, 2008), p. 19, pp. 62–63.

[76] Ibid., p. 19, pp. 62–63.

[77] Research and Markets, 'Clothing & footwear industry market review 2010'; Centre for Retail Research, 'Shopping for Christmas', http://www.retailresearch.org/shoppingforxmas.php, accessed 6 October 2010.

[78] S. Parkinson, 'Climate change and military conflict' (9 November 2008), Scientists for Global Responsibility website, http://www.sgr.org.uk/climate/MAW_Climate_Conflict.pdf, accessed 13 October 2010, p. 6.

[79] B. Parekh, *Gandhi: A very short introduction* (Oxford: Oxford University Press, 1997), pp. 66–67.

[80] Ibid., p. 75.

[81] D. Francis, *Lessons from Kosovo/a: Alternatives to war (the peace testimony in the twenty-first century)* (London: Quaker Peace & Social Witness, 2001).

[82] Stockholm International Peace Research Institute, 'The 15 countries with the highest military expenditure in 2009'.

[83] Extrapolated from World Health Organisation, *World report on violence and health*, ch. 2.

[84] Ibid., p. 3.

[85] Gilligan, *Violence: Reflections on a national epidemic*, p. 111.

[86] C. Batmanghelidjh, *Shattered lives: Children who live with courage and dignity* (London: Jessica Kingsley, 2007).

[87] Gilligan, *Violence: Reflections on a national epidemic*, p. 191.

[88] S. Žižek, *Violence* (London: Profile Books, 2008), p. 2.

[89] L. Tolstoy, *War and peace* (London: Penguin, 1982), p. 1420.

[90] Nott, J in *The Independent*, 23 February 2002.

[91] Thames Television, 'Special presentation section, part II, 4. Hitler's Germany: 1933–1939' in *The world at war* [TV documentary], 1973.

[92] Batmanghelidjh, *Shattered lives*, p. 102.

[93] P. Freire, *Pedagogy of the oppressed* (London: Penguin, 1996), p. 44.

[94] P. Levi, (1988) 'The gray zone' in N. Scheper-Hughes, and P. Bourgois, eds., *Violence in war and peace: An anthology*, p. 85.

[95] Batmanghelidjh, *Shattered lives,* p.103.

[96] S. Milgram, 'Some conditions of obedience and disobedience to authority' in *Human Relations,* 18/1 (1965), pp. 57–76, p. 57, p. 65.

[97] D. Day (1942) in M. E. Jegen, ed., *Words of peace: Selections from the writings of Dorothy Day,* (Erie, PA: Benet Press, 1989), p. 49.

[98] M. Rose, 'How soon could our Army lose a war' in *Daily Telegraph,* 5 April 1998, cited in House of Commons Defence Committee, *Duty of care,* volume 1. London: The Stationery Office, 2005.

[99] Frontline, 'The impact of killing and how to prepare the soldier' (1 March 2005), PBS Frontline: The Soldier's.

[100] M. Rafferty (2000) in Quaker Peace & Social Witness, ed., *Affirming the light: Ten stories of Quaker peace witness* (London: Quaker Peace & Social Witness, 2002), p. 35.

[101] W. Wink, *The powers that be: Theology for a new millennium* (New York: Doubleday, 1998).

[102] H. Arendt (1969) in Scheper-Hughes and P. Bourgois, eds., *Violence in war and peace,* pp. 241–2.

[103] P. Rogers, 'Beyond "liddism": Towards real global security' (1 April 2010), open Democracy website, http://www.opendemocracy.net/paul-rogers/beyond-%E2%80%9Cliddism%E2%80%9D-towards-real-global-security, accessed 23 October 2010.

[104] D. Francis, *From pacification to peacebuilding: A call to global transformation* (London: Pluto, 2010).

[105] T. Hobbes (1651), *Leviathan* (1651), McMaster University Faculty of Social Sciences website, http://socserv.mcmaster.ca/~econ/ugcm/3ll3/hobbes/Leviathan.pdf, accessed 23 October 2010.

[106] W. Penn (1696), 'An essay towards the present and future peace of Europe' in J. Besse, ed., *Essays and belles lettres: Penn's fruits of solitude, & other writings* (London: Everyman, n.d), p. 8.

[107] *Romanian Times,* 'Italian politician compares Roma gypsies to dogs' (10 February 2011), http://www.romaniantimes.at/news/General_News/2011-02-10/13075/_Italian_politician_compares_Roma_gypsies_to_dogs, accessed 12 February 2011.

[108] Cited in J. Barnes (2010), 'Fan rant: Action movies and the girl who loves them' (4 March 2010), Cinematical website, http://blog. moviefone.com/2010/03/04/fan-rant-action-movies-and-the-girl-who-loves-them, accessed 12 February 2011.

[109] A. McIntosh, *Hell and high water: Climate change, hope and the human condition* (Edinburgh: Birlinn, 2008), p. 112.

[110] G. W. Bush, 'Remarks by the President upon arrival' (16 September 2001), The White House website, http://georgewbush-whitehouse. archives.gov/news/releases/2001/09/20010916-2.html, accessed 1 November 2010.

[111] Senior NCO army male in S. Rutherford et al. in *Quantitative & qualitative research into sexual harassment in the armed forces* (London: Equal Opportunities Commission and the Ministry of Defence, 2006), p. 19.

[112] A. Mpunzi, 'Black theology as liberation theology' in Moore, B., ed., *Black theology: The South African voice* (London: Hurst & Co., 1973).

[113] J. Pickard [personal communication].

[114] Extrapolated from IGD (2009), Centre for Retail Research, 'Shopping for Christmas' and Research and Markets, 'Clothing & footwear industry market review 2010'; Office of National Statistics, 'Lifestyles and social participation' (chapter 13) in *Social trends 39*. Newport: ONS, 2009, p. 95.

[115] I. C. Heyward, *Saving Jesus from those who are right: Rethinking what it means to be Christian* (Minneapolis, MN: Fortress, 1999), p. 83; *The redemption of God: A theology of mutual relation* (Lanham, MD: University Press of America, 1982).

[116] R. Craig and J. Mindell eds., *Health Survey for England, 2006: Cardiovascular disease and risk factors* (Leeds: the information centre, 2006), pp. 10–12.

[117] Work Foundation, *The good worker: A survey of attitudes towards work in the UK* (London: Work Foundation, 2006), p. 7.

[118] N. Isles, *The joy of work?* (London: Work Foundation, 2007), p. 7.

[119] Chartered Institute for Personnel and Development, *Employee outlook: Year review* (London: CIPD, 2010), p. 11, 13.

[120] Ofcom, *Communications market report: 2010* (London: Ofcom, 2010), p. 160.

[121] Ibid., p. 175.

[122] National Family Week, Results of an unpublished survey of parents and children obtained directly from NFW, 2010.

[123] World Health Organisation. *World report on violence and health*, p.39. Citing a US study.

[124] BMW cinema advertisement (2009).

[125] S. Palmer in Z. Williams, *The commercialisation of childhood.* (London: Compass, n.d), p. 7.

[126] E. Mayo (2005) in Williams, *The commercialisation of childhood*, p. 6.

[127] A. Phillips, 'The pursuit of happiness is making us miserable' in *The Guardian: Review*, 4 September 2010.

[128] W. Berry, 'Two economies' in B. Keeble, ed., *Every man an artist: Readings in the traditional philosophy of art* (n.p.: World Wisdom, 2005), p. 200.

[129] Greenpeace email, 6 October 2001.

[130] Sax et al. in D. G. Myers, 'The funds, friends and faith of happy people', in American Psychologist, 55/1, (2000), p. 58.

[131] T. Kasser, *The high price of materialism* (Cambridge, MA: MIT Press, 2002); P. Cohen and J. Cohen (1996) in T, Kasser, *The high price of materialism* (Cambridge, MA: MIT Press, 2002), pp. 16–17.

[132] Ibid.

[133] G. Milland and G. Warren, 'Austerity cabinet has 18 millionaires' in *The Sunday Times*, 23 May 2010.

[134] HC. Hansard, 'Comprehensive spending review', column 951, 20 October 2010.

[135] G. Raynor, 'Blair home number nine: £1m house for student daughter' in *Daily Telegraph*, 28 August 2010.

[136] M. Lea, 'Tory MP Viggers admits he is "ashamed and humiliated" over £1,600 duck island claim that "the birds never liked anyway"' in *Daily Mail*, 23 May 2009.

[137] I. Crichton Smith, 'Real people in a real place', p. 20.

138 Personal communication from Campaign Against Arms Trade, 2010.

139 BAE Systems, 'Outstanding performance is found in the natural world. And in ours', http://www.baesystems.com/graduates, accessed 21 October 2010.

140 BBC News, 'Harmless toy or recruiting sergeant?' (3 April 2009), http://news.bbc.co.uk/1/hi/magazine/7978848.stm, accessed 23 October 2010.

141 R. Williams, (2009).

142 K. Lee, (2010) [unpublished].

143 Los Angeles Times, 'The homicide report' (9 November 2010), http://projects.latimes.com/homicide/map, accessed 9 November 2010.

144 D. LaChapelle, Rize [documentary film], Los Angeles: David LaChapelle Studios, 2005.

145 Freire, Pedagogy of the oppressed, p. 26, 29, 30, 66, 75, 84.

146 K. Armstrong, The Bible: The biography (Croydon: Atlantic, 2007), p. 82.

147 Matthew (22:36–40).

148 Augustine, Confessions, (trans. Burton), 12.25.35 in Armstrong, The Bible: The biography, p. 123.

149 I. C. Heyward, The redemption of God: A theology of mutual relation, p. 15.

150 R. Solnit, Hope in the dark: The untold history of people power (revised edn) (Edinburgh: Canongate, 2005), p. 138.

151 Rajagopal (2010) Talk to QPSW Annual Conference, Derbyshire.

152 A. Curle, True justice: Quaker peace makers and peace making (London: Quaker Books, 2007), pp. 28–29.

153 Matthew (22:36–40).

154 J. Macy and M. Young Brown (1998) in Quaker Council for European Affairs, EU sustainable consumption and production action plan: Briefing, evaluation, and action for Quakers (Brussels: QCEA, 2010), p. 32; QPSW Turning the Tide Programme.

155 K. Badie, 'The prayer of humble access' in Churchman, 120/2 (2006), pp. 103–117.

[156] Ibid., p. 108.

[157] Heyward, I C (1989) in L. Tatman, *Knowledge that matters: A feminist theological paradigm and epistemology,* (Sheffield: Sheffield Academic Press, 2001), pp. 197–198.

[158] John (10:10).

[159] B. Thorne, *Person-centred counselling: Therapeutic and spiritual dimensions* (London: Whurr, 1991), p. 90.

[160] M. Gandhi (1984) in T. Merton, ed., *Gandhi on non-violence,* p. 80.

[161] Thich Nhat Hanh, *Touching peace: Practicing the art of mindful living* (Berkeley, CA: Paralax Press, 1992), p. 12.

[162] W. Whitman, *Leaves of grass* (facsimile edn) (New York, 1855), ll. 41–50.

[163] Leviticus (10:25–37).

[164] R. Williams (2009).

[165] Genesis (9:10).

[166] M. Grey, 'Ecomysticism: A contemporary path for Christian healing?' in J. Baxter, ed., *Wounds that heal: Theology, imagination and health* (London: SPCK, 2007).

[167] J. Egware, Make Poverty History campaign, 2007.

[168] Matthew (5:44).

[169] W. Wink, *The powers that be: Theology for a new millennium* (New York: Doubleday, 1998); Matthew (5:38–41); Leviticus (6:29).

[170] L. Gbowee, 'It's time to end Africa's mass rape tragedy' (5 April 2010), The Daily Beast website, http://www.thedailybeast.com/blogs-and-stories/2010-04-05/its-time-to-end-africas-mass-rape-tragedy, accessed 19 March 2011.

[171] Ibid.

[172] H. Arendt (1969) in Scheper-Hughes and P. Bourgois, eds., *Violence in war and peace.*

[173] Curle, *True justice: Quaker peace makers and peace making,* p. 61.

[174] J. C. Arnold, *The lost art of forgiving: Stories of healing from the cancer of bitterness,* (Robertsbridge: Plough, 1998).

[175] Quaker Peace & Social Witness, *Affirming the light,* p. 5.

[176] C. Fager, 'Declaration of war: The hundred-year lamb's war' (30 July 2003), Quaker House website, http://quakerhouse.org/declaration-01.htm, accessed 25 October 2010.

[177] M. Nellis, '"Uprooting the evil in the fields that we know": Reflections on the legacy of and prospects for AVP in the modern world' [unpublished presentation to Alternatives to Violence Project National Gathering], September 2010, p. 9.

[178] H. Marcuse, *One-dimensional man: Studies in the ideology of advanced industrial society* (2nd edn) (London: Routledge, 1991), p. 1.

[179] V. Havel cited in R. Solnit., *Hope in the dark: The untold history of people power* (revised edn), (Edinburgh: Canongate, 2005), p. 66.

[180] R. Johnson (n.d) Talk to Abolition 2000 meeting, London.

[181] W. Penn (1694) *Quaker faith & practice*, 19.45.

[182] J. Punshon, *Portrait in grey: A short history of the Quakers*, (London: Quaker Home Service, 1984), Chapter 1.

[183] D. Boulton, *Militant seedbeds of early Quakerism: Two essays* (Millboro, VA: Quaker Universalist Fellowship, 2005).

[184] 2 Corinthians (1:12).

[185] Dewsbury, W (1655) *Quaker faith & practise*, 19.45.

[186] Ibid., 19.45. [Emphasis added].

[187] Ibid., 19.45. [Emphasis added].

[188] See, for example, M. Jacobs, *Psychodynamic counselling in action* (3rd edn) (London: Sage, 2004).

[189] J. Nayler, *The lamb's war* (1657), Quaker Heritage Press website, http://www.qhpress.org/texts/nayler/lambswar.html, accessed 29 July 2010.

[190] James 4:1 (AV).

[191] *Quaker faith & practice*, 1.02.

[192] G. Fox et al, 'A declaration from the harmless and innocent people of God, called Quakers' (1661), The Religious Society of Friends website, http://www.quaker.org/peaceweb/pdecla07.html, accessed 22 July 2010.

[193] Ibid.

[194] Ibid.

[195] Ibid.

[196] Armstrong, *The Bible: The biography.*

[197] I. Penington, *A question to the professors of Christianity* (1667), Quaker Heritage Press website, http://www.qhpress.org/texts/penington/professors.html, accessed 26 July 2010.

[198] W. Penn (1696), 'An essay towards the present and future peace of Europe' in J. Besse, ed., *Essays and belles lettres: Penn's fruits of solitude, & other writings* (London: Everyman, n.d).

[199] S. L. Cronk, *Peace be with you: A study of the spiritual basis of the Friends peace testimony* (Philadelphia: The Tract Association of Friends, n.d).